# Foreword

Young Writers was established in 1991 and has been passionately devoted to the promotion of reading and writing in children and young adults ever since. The quest continues today. Young Writers remains as committed to the fostering of burgeoning poetic and literary talent as ever.

This year's Young Writers competition has proven as vibrant and dynamic as ever and we are delighted to present a showcase of the best poetry from across the UK. Each poem has been carefully selected from a wealth of *Playground Poets* entries before ultimately being published in this, our thirteenth primary school poetry series.

Once again, we have been supremely impressed by the overall high quality of the entries we have received. The imagination, energy and creativity which has gone into each young writer's entry made choosing the best poems a challenging and often difficult but ultimately hugely rewarding task - the general high standard of the work submitted amply vindicating this opportunity to bring their poetry to a larger appreciative audience.

We sincerely hope you are pleased with our final selection and that you will enjoy *Playground Poets - Scottish Inspirations* for many years to come.

PLAYGROUND POETS

Let your creativity flow...

ode

limerick   haiku

rhyme

ballad

my poems

# - Scottish Inspirations
### Edited by Annabel Cook

 Young**Writers**

First published in Great Britain in 2006 by:
Young Writers
Remus House
Coltsfoot Drive
Peterborough
PE2 9JX
Telephone: 01733 890066
Website: www.youngwriters.co.uk

SB ISBN 1 84602 335 1

# Contents

Nicole Ferguson  (10)          18
David Shedden  (11)            18
Laura McDonald  (11)           19
Brendan Hay  (11)              19
William Robson  (11)           19
David Walker  (11)             20
Jessica Cameron  (10)          20
Kieran Campbell  (11)          20
Jay Keggans  (10)              21
Rebecca Hodge  (10)            21
Arfa Nasir  (10)               21
Ashleigh Dickie  (10)          22

## Claypotts Castle Primary School, Dundee

Steven Hutchison  (10)         22
Mariam Kassam  (10)            22
Nadia Simpson  (10)            23
Roy Macaskill  (10)            23
Louise Dunn  (9)               23
Gemma Hutchison  (10)          24
Bradley Skelly  (11)           24
Jamie Lowrey  (10)             24
Rachel Cameron  (11)           25
Gavin Lee Thomson  (10)        25
Keira Ann Duff  (10)           25
Natalie Smith  (11)            26
Sam Gillan Whyte  (11)         26
Tayler Anderson  (11)          27
Hinna Kassam  (11)             27
Duncan Gillon  (11)            28
Nicola Forbes  (9)             28
Angela Scott  (10)             28
Emma Burnett  (10)             29
Taylor Smart  (10)             29
Rebecca Lindsay  (10)          29
Frankie Moran  (11)            30
Stewart Cowie  (10)            30
Iain Sandeman  (10)            30
Drew Mill  (10)                31
Caitlyn Mooney  (10)           31
Shannon Livingstone  (9)       31

| | |
|---|---|
| Christine Smith  (10) | 32 |
| Sam Dickson  (10) | 32 |
| Caroline Milne  (10) | 32 |
| Morven McGregor  (10) | 33 |
| Dale Grier  (10) | 33 |
| Allan McNicol  (10) | 33 |
| Bobbie Sandeman  (9) | 34 |
| Chloe Anderson  (10) | 34 |
| Lori Allan  (9) | 34 |
| Hannah Fisher  (9) | 35 |
| Andrew Cowie  (10) | 35 |
| Danielle Crawford  (9) | 35 |
| Ryan Webster  (11) | 36 |
| Courtney Roache  (10) | 36 |
| Rachael Lyall  (10) | 36 |
| Dyllon Jeffrey  (10) | 37 |
| Shaun Hendry  (10) | 37 |
| Javed Din  (9) | 37 |
| Kiera Cartmill  (11) | 38 |

## Cults Primary School, Cults

| | |
|---|---|
| Hannah Burt  (9) | 39 |
| Tegan Seivwright  (9) | 40 |
| Fiona Thompson  (10) | 40 |
| Lucy Smith  (10) | 41 |
| Eilidh Scott  (10) | 41 |
| Eve Norris  (9) | 42 |
| Trishna Raj  (10) | 43 |
| Atlanta Taylor Hearns  (9) | 43 |

## Drumbowie Primary School, Falkirk

| | |
|---|---|
| Ailsa Goldie  (10) | 44 |
| Hayley Walker  (10) | 44 |
| Abbie McLean  (9) | 45 |
| Eilidh Park  (7) | 45 |
| Hannah Crawford  (8) | 46 |
| Kelly Montgomery  (7) | 47 |

## Dunecht School, Westhill

| | |
|---|---:|
| Rhea Shearer  (11) | 47 |
| Caroline Sim  (10) | 48 |
| Calum Rae  (10) | 48 |
| Amber Dawson  (11) | 49 |
| Alan McCombie  (11) | 49 |
| Hayley O'Brien  (10) | 50 |
| Caitlin Drummond  (10) | 51 |
| Kenneth MacBeath  (10) | 52 |
| Kerryn McRae  (10) | 53 |
| Hannah Johnston  (10) | 53 |
| Kyla Hislop  (10) | 54 |
| Finlay McPherson  (9) | 54 |
| Monique Hendy  (9) | 55 |
| Joanna Cook  (10) | 56 |
| Scott Campbell  (10) | 57 |
| Daniel Wilson  (8) | 58 |
| Stephen Hugh Will  (8) | 59 |
| Skye Dawson  (9) | 60 |
| Cameron Brownie  (9) | 61 |
| Philip Oakes  (9) | 62 |

## Easdale Primary School, Oban

| | |
|---|---:|
| Davie Campbell  (9) | 62 |
| Gillian MacKechnie  (9) | 63 |
| Jenny Case  (9) | 63 |
| Sam Nichols  (10) | 64 |
| Rebekah Freya Stephenson  (9) | 65 |
| Hannah Croucher  (10) | 66 |
| Gordon Phillips  (10) | 67 |
| Megan Gilroy  (11) | 68 |
| Holly Wesley  (8) | 69 |

## Eastbank Primary School, Shettleston

| | |
|---|---:|
| Daryl Coutts  (10) | 69 |
| Jaye Brownlie  (11) | 70 |
| Dale Matthews  (11) | 70 |
| Natalie Colvin  (11) | 71 |
| Tyler McNeill  (10) | 71 |
| Darren Currie  (11) | 72 |

| | |
|---|---:|
| Nathan Spencer (10) | 72 |
| Erin Lilley (10) | 73 |
| Hayley Grant (10) | 73 |
| Lewis King (11) | 74 |
| David James Hendry (10) | 75 |
| Aimee Munro (10) | 76 |
| Gillian Ross (11) | 76 |
| Courtney Leigh Williamson (11) | 77 |
| Nichola Mulheron (11) | 77 |
| Jade Freeman (10) | 78 |
| Emily Meechan (11) | 78 |
| Danielle Elizabith Alexander (10) | 79 |
| Jade Stirling (10) | 79 |
| Nicola Wilson (11) | 80 |
| Alexander Coulter (11) | 81 |
| Hayley McIntyre (11) | 82 |

## Gateside Primary School, By Beith

| | |
|---|---:|
| Erin Shepherd (11) | 82 |
| Wesley Smith (9) | 83 |
| Megan Reid (11) | 83 |
| Scott Gillan (11) | 84 |
| Heather Gibson (8) | 84 |
| Fabian Goldie (8) | 85 |
| George McConnell (10) | 85 |
| Nicole Barker (10) | 86 |
| Mollie Kerr (9) | 86 |
| Kayleigh Brown (9) | 87 |
| Rosie McKinney (10) | 87 |
| Emma Reid (9) | 88 |
| Hazel Munro (10) | 88 |
| Graeme Dowie (9) | 89 |
| Sam Warnock (10) | 89 |
| Aneesah Sheikh (8) | 90 |
| Nicola Watson (9) | 91 |

## Kennoway Primary School, Kennoway

| | |
|---|---:|
| Nathan Band (10) | 91 |
| David Halliday (9) | 91 |
| Megan Malcolmson (10) | 92 |
| Rebecca McBeath (10) | 92 |

| | |
|---|---|
| Leona Dodds  (10) | 93 |
| Courtney Mackie  (10) | 93 |
| Luke Hutchison  (10) | 93 |
| Amy Henderson  (9) | 94 |
| Kathleen Allen  (9) | 94 |
| Marnie Lawson  (10) | 94 |

## Kinellar Primary School, Blackburn

| | |
|---|---|
| Erin Smith  (9) | 95 |
| Joanne Findlay  (9) | 95 |
| Lauren Tate  (10) | 95 |
| Shaun MacLeod  (8) | 96 |
| Bryce McLernon  (10) | 96 |
| Alister Logie  (9) | 96 |
| Rhea Barclay  (9) | 97 |
| Victoria Greig  (9) | 97 |
| Holly Pirie  (9) | 97 |
| Douglas Park  (9) | 98 |
| Gavin McKenzie  (10) | 98 |
| Liam Watson  (10) | 98 |
| Alexander Knapper  (9) | 99 |
| Martin Thomson  (10) | 99 |
| Craig Turriff  (10) | 99 |
| Haley Robertson  (8) | 100 |
| James Emslie  (10) | 100 |
| Kourtnay Wood  (9) | 100 |
| Marci Harmati  (9) | 101 |
| David Singer  (10) | 101 |
| Harley Ross  (10) | 101 |
| Anna Moir  (9) | 102 |
| Chloë Matthews  (9) | 102 |
| Jamie Grimbley  (10) | 102 |
| Ruth Ann Bryce  (9) | 103 |
| Tarran Eve Ross  (8) | 103 |
| Ailsa Macdonald  (9) | 104 |
| Hannah Thomson  (9) | 104 |
| Jordan Baxter  (8) | 105 |
| Rowan Smith  (10) | 105 |
| Rebecca Craigmile  (10) | 106 |
| Claire Mitchell  (10) | 106 |
| Fergus Milne  (9) | 106 |

| | |
|---|---|
| Ruth Elias | 129 |
| Andrew James Grant-Suttie  (8) | 129 |
| Heather Oberlander  (8) | 130 |
| Beth Lauder  (8) | 130 |
| Cameron Robertson  (8) | 131 |
| Eoin Patrick  (8) | 131 |
| Joshua Stewart  (8) | 132 |
| Sophie Ferguson  (8) | 132 |
| Esther Borsi  (7) | 132 |
| Abigail Pooley  (7) | 133 |
| Matthew Watt  (8) | 133 |
| Adam Naylor  (8) | 133 |
| Isla Menneer  (8) | 134 |
| Thomas Brogden  (7) | 134 |
| Hamish Barbour  (8) | 134 |
| Michael Hagan  (8) | 135 |
| Riccardo Cucchi  (8) | 135 |

## Leslie Primary School, Leslie

| | |
|---|---|
| Jade Munro  (8) | 135 |
| Carla Blakey  (9) | 135 |
| Rachel Gould  (9) | 136 |
| Kirsty Drysdale  (9) | 136 |
| Chloe McCaffery  (9) | 136 |
| Lilybeth Paterson  (8) | 136 |
| Evie Cumming  (9) | 137 |
| Keiren Martin  (9) | 137 |
| Akram Basha  (9) | 137 |
| Amy Gordon  (9) | 137 |

## Maud School, Maud

| | |
|---|---|
| Lydia Stephen  (9) | 138 |
| James Scott  (7) | 138 |
| Jody McGregor  (7) | 138 |
| Kelsey Burnett  (11) | 139 |
| Aimee Mowat  (7) | 139 |
| Kelly Paterson  (11) | 139 |
| Cameron Buchan  (9) | 140 |
| Stephanie-Louise Wilson  (7) | 140 |
| Ela McDougall  (7) | 140 |
| Iain Birnie  (10) | 141 |

| | |
|---|---|
| Faye Cruickshank  (9) | 141 |
| Megan Will  (9) | 141 |
| Alexander Paterson  (9) | 142 |
| Jasmine Matthews  (10) | 142 |
| Matthew Paterson  (11) | 142 |
| James Greig  (10) | 143 |
| James Hay  (10) | 143 |
| Ryan Cameron  (11) | 144 |
| Sam Graham  (7) | 144 |

## Mile End Primary School, Aberdeen

| | |
|---|---|
| Rachael Robertson  (11) | 144 |
| Sarah Rahman  (10) | 145 |
| Scott Mackie  (11) | 146 |
| Finlay Johnston  (11) | 146 |
| Kenneth Will  (10) | 147 |
| Nicholas Logan  (11) | 147 |
| Ellen Shand  (10) | 148 |
| Matthew John Greer (11) | 149 |
| Sammy Anindo  (11) | 150 |
| David Hewitt  (11) | 150 |
| Keira Napier  (11) | 151 |
| Connor Anderson  (11) | 151 |
| Campbell Simpson  (10) | 152 |
| Cameron Howe  (10) | 153 |
| Clare Armstrong  (10) | 154 |
| Joseph Lawson  (10) | 155 |
| Murray Gauld  (11) | 155 |
| Melissa Smart  (11) | 156 |
| Gavin Thomas  (10) | 157 |
| Mugdha Nagrath  (11) | 158 |

## Rattray Primary School, Rattray

| | |
|---|---|
| Jennifer Ramsay  (9) | 158 |
| Jamie Mckinlay  (10) | 159 |
| Jonathan Kermath  (10) | 159 |
| Christie Comrie  (9) | 160 |
| Melissa Harper  (9) | 161 |
| Wayne Osborne  (11) | 162 |
| Connor Buchanan  (10) | 163 |
| Robert Willemars  (10) | 164 |

| Jack Bruce (10) | 165 |
| Cara Henderson (9) | 166 |
| Hannah Ingham (10) | 167 |
| Gregor Thomas (9) | 168 |
| Sarah Small (10) | 168 |

## St Dominic's RC Primary School, Crieff

| Laura Clegg (11) | 169 |
| Merissa De Lange (11) | 169 |
| Ashley O'Neill (11) | 170 |
| Christopher Bendall (11) | 170 |
| Callum Anderson (11) | 171 |
| Benedict Robinson (11) | 171 |
| Morven McGuigan (11) | 172 |
| Charlotte Macdonald (11) | 173 |
| Kirsty Maclean (10) | 174 |
| Michael Addley (11) | 175 |
| Roslyn Ward (11) | 175 |
| Bobby Garforth (11) | 176 |
| Eliot Johnstone (11) | 176 |
| Hannah McAuley (11) | 177 |
| Joel Welch (11) | 177 |
| Jessica Wake (11) | 178 |

## St Peter's RC Primary School, Dalbeattie

| Louise Pickthall (11) | 178 |
| Chanice McLean (11) | 179 |
| Ashlie Broll (12) | 179 |
| Fraser Drummond (11) | 180 |
| Fraser Gray (9) | 181 |
| Rhianna Rae (10) | 182 |
| Mhairi Valentine (10) | 183 |

## Saline Primary School, Saline

| Danielle McIntosh (10) | 184 |
| Calum Leask (11) | 185 |
| Eilidh Moyes (11) | 185 |
| Sophie Jeffrey (10) | 186 |
| Alex Monk (11) | 186 |
| Robbie Gordon (11) | 187 |

| Lewis Kerr (11) | 187 |
| Sean Sutherland (11) | 188 |
| Ryan Watson (11) | 188 |
| Aimee Aird (11) | 189 |
| Joe Butler (11) | 189 |
| Kenna Grantham (11) | 190 |

## Stanley Primary School, Ardrossan

| Rebekah Wallace (9) | 190 |
| Kimberly Pringle (9) | 190 |
| Sarah-Jane Howie (8) | 191 |
| Lee McIntosh (8) | 191 |
| Jordan Gray (9) | 191 |
| Mark Coyle (10) | 192 |
| Kirsty Skene (10) | 192 |
| Rebekka Muir (9) | 193 |
| Kerkyra Kantas Davis (10) | 193 |
| Nicola Hind (9) | 194 |
| Jordan Watt (9) | 194 |
| Ashleigh Myers (9) | 195 |
| Sarah-Jayne Meek (10) | 195 |
| Gordon Wallace (9) | 196 |
| Matthew Duff (9) | 196 |
| Aimee Ferguson (9) | 197 |
| Linda Young (9) | 197 |
| Connie Bailey (10) | 198 |
| Alexander MacLaren (10) | 198 |
| Craig Munn (10) | 199 |
| Paige Russell (9) | 199 |
| Gavin Lundy (9) | 200 |
| Jena Montgomerie (8) | 200 |
| Lisa Barraclough (8) | 200 |
| Marcus McCrindle (9) | 201 |
| Danielle Gilmour (8) | 201 |
| Rachael McMullan (9) | 201 |
| Alannah Bailey (9) | 202 |
| Lauren Lynch (9) | 202 |
| Georgie McDougall (8) | 202 |
| Rachel Blades (8) | 203 |
| Drue Lauren Brown (9) | 203 |
| Jonathan Muir (8) | 203 |

Shaun Jackson  (8)                                    204
Carly Morris  (8)                                     204
Craig Mackay  (9)                                     204
Emma Steven  (10)                                     205
Nathan Lee Wieringa  (9)                              205
Gemma Dunlop  (10)                                    206

## Strachan Primary School, Banchory
Sarah Middleton  (11)                                 206
Oliver Middleton  (8)                                 207
Joanne Stewart  (9)                                   207
Ryan Neish  (11)                                      208
Cameron Randalls  (10)                                208
Beatrice Reader  (9)                                  208
Robert Stroud  (11)                                   209
Amy Balfour  (10)                                     209
Douglas Law  (10)                                     209
Martha Collier  (10)                                  210
Stuart Gray  (9)                                      210
Adam Castle  (10)                                     210

## Strathkinness Primary School, Strathkinness
Lewis Wedderburn  (10)                                211
Craig Bayne  (10)                                     211
Heather Walker  (11)                                  212
Joseph Gibbins  (10)                                  212
Adam Murray  (11)                                     213
Robert Jarvis  (10)                                   213
Coral Jackson  (11)                                   214
Alan Sunter  (10)                                     215
Evie Paterson  (10)                                   216
Paul Sinclair  (9)                                    217
Callum Barclaywood  (9)                               218
Tamara Levy  (10)                                     218
Fin Jones  (10)                                       219
Jennifer Wood  (10)                                   219
Lindsey White  (10)                                   220

## Tannadice Primary School, Forfar

| | |
|---|---|
| Shaina Sanderson  (9) | 220 |
| Anna Kidd  (8) | 221 |
| Alia Kelly  (9) | 221 |
| Kirsten Doyle  (9) | 221 |
| Ryan Farquharson  (10) | 222 |
| Ruth Moore  (9) | 222 |
| Cheryl Williams  (9) | 222 |
| Alana Edwards  (9) | 223 |
| Christopher George  (9) | 223 |
| Callum Dunleavy  (9) | 223 |
| Molly Wilson  (9) | 224 |
| Emily Baillie  (9) | 224 |
| Araminta Yates  (9) | 224 |
| Gemma Mackintosh  (9) | 225 |
| Ruth Mayes  (9) | 225 |
| Dylan Simpson  (10) | 225 |
| Megan Barclay  (9) | 226 |
| Craig Joiner  (9) | 226 |
| Laura Herd  (9) | 226 |
| John Gibb  (10) | 227 |

## Tarland Primary School, Tarland

| | |
|---|---|
| Gillean Palmer  (7) | 227 |
| Eilidh Anderson  (8) | 227 |
| Halla Price  (10) | 228 |
| Ellie Palmer  (10) | 229 |
| Ishbel Rosie Price  (8) | 229 |
| Emer Cunningham  (8) | 230 |
| Arlene Jenkins  (8) | 230 |
| Sarah Preston  (8) | 230 |
| Jade Whitaker  (9) | 231 |

## Victoria Primary School, Airdrie

| | |
|---|---|
| Megan Andrew  (10) | 231 |
| George Gordon  (10) | 232 |
| Chloe Robertson  (11) | 232 |
| Craig Lafferty  (11) | 233 |
| Amy Priest  (11) | 233 |
| Gordon Allan  (10) | 234 |

# The Poems

# Tolerance

Tolerance is to care
It also makes you play fair
I feel tolerance is really good
Follow it, I think people should.

Intolerance is really bad
It could make people very sad
Sometimes when I go to play
They tell me to go away.

All together all day
Why don't we all go and play?
Black, white do not fight
It's just a game *all right!*

**John Opfer  (12)**


# Loch Charkan

As I look out my bedroom window I see Loch Charkan
Glinting in the sunlight, walled off by rocky mountains.
On the mountain's scree forms a fiery dragon.
The loch itself is a gateway to a watery world.
Out of it the River Albannach flows.
The loch is as grey as an elephant.
In the wind, waves plume up like white and grey horses.

The dragon in the scree scorches bracken red in the autumn
As it guards a pass into the mountains.

A dinosaur can clearly be seen beside the dragon.
The two creatures help the rowan tree, a magic tree which
                                             repels witches.
As well as this, the rowan feeds birds with its red berries.

The grey thin road snakes alongside Charkan
As it sparkles in the vast countryside around her
Bright like a crystal, shining in a midnight world.

**Holly Gray  (8)**
**Achfary Primary School, Lairg**

# Loch Cosmarium

As I gaze out of my living room window
I see Loch Cosmarium.
It is slate-grey, matching the colour of my roof.
The loch is a rough, irregular oval.
It is a blue jelly, disturbed by a monster underneath.
Boats float on it, like white bananas.

In this wilderness, rivers have carved steep-side gullies
As if a sharp knife has opened with a slice, the mountain's face.
In 10,000 years, will we have a Grand Canyon?
I'll be long dead.
The loch is enclosed by these mountains in a great coliseum.

Floating in the black depths are tiny organisms called desmids.
It is their watery home.

The rushes lining the loch, look like hairs on a stubby beard, sharp
and pointed.

I walk down the rocky path to the edge of the loch.
I bend down, search for the flattest, smoothest stone,
Pull my arms backwards and with a flick, let it go.
Watching, counting as it skims the surface until it sinks beneath
Loch Cosmarium.

**Patrick Gray (8)**
**Achfary Primary School, Lairg**

# The Loch Beside My House

As I look out my kitchen window I see a loch.
It looks like a long head with only one ear.
It is a baby-blue shade with white lines wiggling across it.
It is like a blue jelly sprayed with wriggles of cream and
Bits of wood like chocolate sprinkles, floating on top.

The mountains, like sleeping dinosaurs, their skin coloured brown,
Yellow, green and grey surround the loch.
The chameleon's tongue stretches round the end of the loch.

The graveyard sits on the side of the loch.
It's old and horrible.
Some of the gravestones have fallen over, they don't have
good balance.
It has weeds.
It hasn't any flowers like nice graveyards.
Imagine that!

**Claire Barnes-Miller  (8)**
**Achfary Primary School, Lairg**


# A Soldier In The War

*I see . . .*
Dead people covered in blood.
Germans shooting at us with all the ammo they've got.
My gun is slipping with the sweat on my hands
And bullets are coming at me like bolts of lightning.
Soldiers running in our freezing cold uniforms which we have to wear.
Hitler giving the orders to attack us, or to fire at will.
The dog-tags that have come off when the soldiers have died.
Planes dropping bombs on the faraway town.

*I feel . . .*
Angry like being captured by the Germans or
Mad because your friend was killed by the Germans.
Scared because your friend was killed
So you're next on the list!

**Fraser Arnott  (11)**
**Airlie Primary School, Airlie**

# A Soldier In The War

*I feel . . .*
My heavy rifle in my sweaty hand,
and the rest of the army brushing against me,
as the whole army marches over the land,
I can feel the painful stings from a bee.
My sweaty uniform sticking to my body,
as if I'm a nobody.
There's cold thick blood pouring from my hand,
dripping on the poor men who have died.
My chest, pumping like a pump for a car with a puncture.
The vibrations as the bombs hit the ground.

*I hear . . .*
The commander shouting the battle plan.
Gunfire and the ear-splitting screaming of people dying
and the shouting of an injured man.
The sound of the planes is like a drill through my head.

*I see . . .*
The German aircraft flying in the sky,
The dirty track in front of me.
A huge city with some of it on fire,
Bombs and torpedoes dropping from the sky.

**William James Callum Batty (9)**
**Airlie Primary School, Airlie**


# A Soldier In The War

I'm a soldier in the war in tanks fighting for,
fighting for country and wives.
In my tank I see big flashing bombs,
enemy forces coming towards me firing their rifles,
shouting, screaming and yelling.
It's so hard to concentrate, like I'm losing my mind.
I feel the tank's steering wheel, heavy in my hands.

**David Elder (11)**
**Airlie Primary School, Airlie**

# Life In The Blitz

*I see . . .*
Big clouds of smoke and firemen pulling people out of the rubble.
The rubble is like big bits of confetti.
Wrecked cars and buildings come crumbling down like crumbs falling
from a biscuit and bombs hitting the ground.

*I hear . . .*
Air raid sirens like a cat miaowing,
Guns shooting, like a running crowd of people.
Planes are flying by with a droning noise drilling
right through my head.

*I feel . . .*
The dust from the buildings that have fallen down and
My mum hugging me tightly.
When the bombs drop, the ground shakes
and makes me shiver.

**Brogan McGowan  (9)**
**Airlie Primary School, Airlie**

# An Evacuee

*I see . . .*
Hills, trees, funny things that look like cotton wool
and trains coming back from the country,
children crying, cuddling into their brothers and sisters.

*I hear . . .*
Crying, the train goes *clickerty-click,* the hullabaloo,
like the chatter before a film starts at the cinema.

*I feel . . .*
My sister's small, sweaty hands, I feel excited
but the butterflies in my tummy say I'm nervous.

**Alice Doig  (10)**
**Airlie Primary School, Airlie**

# A Soldier In The War

*I see . . .*
Soldiers dying who have real passion for their country.
There's a rumble in the foreground as tanks erupt,
shooting at Churchill's army.
Our spitfires rumble over from England to defeat
Hitler's army, with ease.
The trench across from us caving in, with real landslide looks.
U-boats turning back to Germany because they know
they will die.

*I hear . . .*
Rifles shooting like a dart hitting the dartboard
with a massive thud.
The scream of a soldier with a torturous death.
Myself breathing vigorously with a scared content.
The rumble of German bombers drilling through my ears.
There's a temptation telling me to get out of my trench
and shoot at all the tanks I can.

*I feel . . .*
So tempted to run like a horse and shoot all the Germans I can,
The raindrops pounding off my hair like a boxer receiving blows
in a boxing match.
The mud squidging in and out of my boots,
I get the feeling that I'm going to die.
There is a nerve-racking feeling that will
win the war for Britain.
A spine-chilling nerve of fear drips down my spine.
Germany will fall like bricks and tumble to the ground.

**Kieran Dunn  (11)**
**Airlie Primary School, Airlie**

# The Show

Sitting in my bomb shelter, I see no war,
I see no fighting,
I see the most fantastic show.

I see the erupting explosion of falling bombs
like the breathtaking fireworks, dancing in the sky.
Surrounding are the planes, diving and falling like confetti.

The hands of my mum holding me cosy
settle me in my theatre seat.

I hear the familiar tune of the air raid siren,
act as background music to the opera singer,
like the sad scream of a lost child.

I see clouds, as I see feathers,
levitating themselves in the black scene,
being imagined from a blackout.

The walking footsteps vibrate the stage
as the walking hurriedly becomes a frantic,
panicky run.

Finally, the grand finale comes.
The explosions, screams, the confetti getting even closer.
The bang, the blast, the gold dust sprinkling over my head
like the sand from my sandbag, protecting our lives.

Then all of a sudden, the lights go out,
the screaming stops, the curtains shut, black.
The show is over, it is all over.

**Rosy Duncan  (11)**
**Airlie Primary School, Airlie**

# A Soldier In The War

*I see . . .*
Sparks coming from bombs.
Clouds of thick black smoke like a mushroom.
All smashed planes like a toy chewed up by a dog.

*I feel . . .*
Bullets are like darts in my arm,
A cold breeze on my face.
Scared and tired, I dream of home.

*I hear . . .*
People moaning,
Guns are banging.
Bombers' engines
Air raid sirens.

*I taste . . .*
The blood in my mouth,
The smoke in my mouth.

**Sean Grant  (9)**
**Airlie Primary School, Airlie**


# A Soldier In The War

*I can see . . .*
Bombs as they hit the ground like a scattering of birds,
Fire like the city has been lit up.
Smoke like thick grey clouds.
Soldiers marching into battle.

*I can feel . . .*
My gun like a metal pole
Slipping out of my hand.

*I can hear . . .*
Gunfire like a low note on a piano.
The bombs coming down
Like an old lady's scream.

**Steven Murphy  (8)**
**Airlie Primary School, Airlie**

# Life In The Blitz

*I see . . .*
The explosions like fireworks.
The blackness covers the whole of Germany
all day and all night.
There are streams of bombs, pouring down.
The sky is covered with black planes,
like bats swarming amongst the big grey
haze of clouds.

*I hear . . .*
The bombs pouring down like a rainforest storm.
People are screaming,
their houses have been bombed.

*I feel . . .*
Alone, and I am the only one left in the world.
I am scared because I don't know if my dad
is ever coming home.

**Sian Duncan  (9)**
**Airlie Primary School, Airlie**


# A Soldier In The War

*I see . . .*
People with lost limbs like gerbils without tails,
Craters like where you plant plants
Burning trees like candles, burning in the night.

*I hear . . .*
Boots on the ground as the titanium lads
march into battle.

*I taste . . .*
The blood in my mouth, it tastes like metal and the
bad taste of war remains for ever in your soul, forever.

**David Thomson  (9)**
**Airlie Primary School, Airlie**

# The Evacuee

*I see . . .*
Mum waving goodbye, I think she's going to cry,
People waving and sobbing as if someone's about to die.
The city flashing past, this might be the last!
Fields flash past, like a slide show on fields,
The night sky with flashes like searchlights, lighting up
                                        the evening bliss.
Frothy waterfalls like memories of when my family went to a river
And splashed in the mild waters,
I am worried and confused, I don't know if I will ever
See my mum again!

*I feel . . .*
The fresh air swirling around me like witches' fingers
Curling around my body.
My teddy's soft fur brushing against me as I remember
The blur of the war.
My face tenses as tears trickle down my face.
Butterflies flutter in my tummy as the train
Chugs faster and faster.

*I hear . . .*
My heart thumping as I get farther away from the city,
As I think of my little kitty.
Children crying, as I look for the planes flying to the city.
The crunch of my biscuit as it crumbles
Whilst my tummy rumbles
The faint sound of bombs in the city.
I feel scared and uneven,
I just wish the train could turn around and go back home
So I could see my mum. I just wish!

**Anna Bannerman  (11)**
**Airlie Primary School, Airlie**

# A Bad Childhood!

*I see . . .*
Other children crying with their gas masks on the string
in their small boxes.
Crying mums are soon going to make a puddle with their salty tears.

*I hear . . .*
The word goodbye, over and over in my head,
It's nearly piercing my head.
Screaming bombs dropping from the sky
And lots of hubble-bubble talk of where we're going.

*I smell . . .*
Steam from the train starting to warm up,
The crumbly biscuits crunching in my mouth.

*I feel . . .*
A slippery suitcase handle like a slippery snake,
A tear slipping down my cheek like a cold tap drilling,
A fluttering label round my neck is like a graceful butterfly.

**Rowan Ishbel Corrigan  (9)**
**Airlie Primary School, Airlie**


# A Soldier In The War

As I come out of a trench, I see dead bodies
Like carcasses in the back of a butcher's shop,
Bullets slicing through the air.
A tank, mighty and bold.
There are people dying all around me.

I feel an excruciating pain in my hand
I look, I have a hole in my hand!
The sand hits my face like pelting rain,
I shoot German soldiers as I run.
I get a grenade, I throw it and duck -
I hear the boom.

**Rudi Kinmont  (8)**
**Airlie Primary School, Airlie**

# Life In The Blitz

*I see . . .*
Huge bombs on houses. People wearing gas masks.
People screaming and scurrying into their bomb shelters like ants.
Aeroplanes circling above the houses with bombs coming down.
Dead bodies on the ground, the black sky. Fire everywhere.

*I feel . . .*
The rubble coming from the roof,
The ground vibrating when the bombs drop.
My mum cuddling me.
When the bombs are dropping I feel terrified

*I hear . . .*
Bombs making an enormous bang,
People screaming and crying.
Aeroplanes zooming about in the sky, like thunder.

**Mhairi Duncan (9)**
**Airlie Primary School, Airlie**

# Evacuee

*I feel . . .*
The rough seat like an elephant's back,
Sweat dropping off my hands like rain.
My biscuit crumbling in my mouth like a leaf rustling.
The space, the open air.

*I hear . . .*
People laughing like they don't care about war.
My heart thumping like I'm out of breath,
Children crying for help,
The train whizzing along the track.

*I see . . .*
The purple heathered hills go flashing by,
The trees crashing together like shots going off.
The sun beating down hard on my face.
Birds flying to safety, like me.

**Lauren McLean (10)**
**Airlie Primary School, Airlie**

# Life In The Blitz

*I can see . . .*
Houses collapsing like an invisible heavy weight
Has fallen from the sky on them,
People screaming, crying for help like the air raid siren.
People dying like from the click of a switch.
Big grey clouds, like someone has come along and coloured them in
With a felt tipped pen
Bombs dropping like a ball dropping in a football match.

*I can hear . . .*
The air raid siren drilling right through my painful head,
Trains leaving the city, breaking my eardrums.
Police cars driving round and round with their sirens on looking like
They're chasing each other.
People chattering like an enormous shower.

*I can feel . . .*
The bullets firing in and out through bodies,
I feel like I'm the only one still alive in the war.
The air raid siren sending shivers right through my body to my brain.
My heart beating faster than ever with trepidation.

**Jack Easson  (10)**
**Airlie Primary School, Airlie**


# A D-Day Soldier

I see boats flipped over like toy boats on the pond,
Shot soldiers all over the ground like dominoes, scattered everywhere.
I hear *tat-tat-tat* of German guns from the pillboxes on the ragged hills
I feel my kitbag like a pile of bricks on my back,
My rifle's heavy in my hand.

**Cameron McFadden  (9)**
**Airlie Primary School, Airlie**

# The Evacuee

*I see . . .*
Trains that are giant black and white,
houses that are black and grey.
Lots of people; mums and dads
grans and grandads crying and hugging,
talking and laughing.

*I feel . . .*
My thick socks itching me like mad,
I feel sad, like when I lost my teddy.
I feel the handle of my suitcase,
it is rough, like a piece of wood.

*I taste . . .*
Salty tears dripping down my face
like it is raining.

*I hear . . .*
Lots of voices,
I hear someone crying like a dog.
I hear the train puffing into the station.

**Jamie Reynolds  (9)**
**Airlie Primary School, Airlie**

# The Evacuee

*I can see . . .*
Cows grazing in the fields as we go flashing by
A muddy farmyard next to a big farmhouse,
Big green hills like a monster rising in the distance,
Children playing in their gardens scuttling like mice.

*I can feel . . .*
My rough, heavy suitcase in my hand
The hot air from the bright yellow sun
People nudging me with their sharp elbows
The soft smooth seat against my back.

*I can hear . . .*
Mums talking like mice squeaking,
The loud noise of the train that goes *clickety-clack!*
The noise of the wind whirling around in the sky,
Babies roaring for their mums.
Children munching their biscuits.

**Isla Millar  (9)**
**Airlie Primary School, Airlie**


# My Mum

My mum is bright pink,
She is the first day of spring
In a field of beautiful flowers.
She is like the sun,
She is a pair of jeans and a comfy couch.
She is Trisha,
And a big bowl of ice cream.

**Ryan McCreadie  (11)**
**Barshare Primary School, Cumnock**

# My Teacher

My teacher is a vibrant yellow
She is a warm spring day
In a breezy park
She is sunny and bright
She is high heels and a skirt
And a comfy coach
She is 'Who Wants To Be A Millionaire?'
And a bowl of sticky toffee pudding.

**Rachael Hewitson  (10)**
**Barshare Primary School, Cumnock**


# My Little Brother John

My little brother is baby blue
He is a cool summer breeze
On a lovely sandy beach.
He is cool and breezy, swishing around
He is a pair of trainers
And a nice soft chair
He is a Power Ranger
And a nice warm cup of tea.

**Gillian Bradford  (10)**
**Barshare Primary School, Cumnock**


# My Teacher

My teacher is sparkly gold
And a hot summer day
In a nice hot bath.
She is a hot summer breeze,
She is a lovely dress.
She is a big comfy couch,
She is 'Coronation Street',
And a drink of Cocoa.

**Anne Muir  (11)**
**Barshare Primary School, Cumnock**

## My Sister Sam

My sister is mustard with black dots
She is a cold everlasting winter
In a lonely ghost town
She is lightning, as it strikes
She is a torn dress
And a smashed television
She is 'Midsomer Murders'
And a piece of mouldy cheese.

**Ben Donaldson  (10)**
**Barshare Primary School, Cumnock**


## My Mum

My mum is light brown,
She is a spring morning
In a garden of flowers.
She is a cool breeze,
She is a long red dress
And a cream leather couch.
She is 'Emmerdale'
And a delicious steak pie.

**Brian Bell  (11)**
**Barshare Primary School, Cumnock**


## My Aunty Jack

My aunty Jack is red
She is winter, walking
Through the woods and
A cold stormy night with
Ragged cloth.
She is 'The Bill'
With a hot bowl of soup.

**Jordan Hastings  (10)**
**Barshare Primary School, Cumnock**

# My Friend

Emma is bright pink
She is a warm summer's day in Ibiza
She is sunny and bright
She is a big fluffy coat
And a comfy coach
She is SpongeBob Squarepants
And a plate of pudding.

**Natalie Burns (10)**
**Barshare Primary School, Cumnock**

# My Big Sister

My big sister is black
She is a cool winter morning
In the cold park.
She is a thunderstorm
She is a sweatshirt
And an untidy bed.
She is an 'Egg Heads'
And a plate of cold spaghetti.

**Nicole Ferguson (10)**
**Barshare Primary School, Cumnock**

# My Teacher

My teacher is dark
She is a stormy night
In the rough sea.
She is a whirlwind,
She is a grey skirt.
She is a messy desk,
She is 'Emmerdale'
She is a warm tin of corn.

**David Shedden (11)**
**Barshare Primary School, Cumnock**

## My Sister

My sister is a gloomy red,
She is a cool summer's breeze
On a lovely warm beach where the tide is calm.
She is a cold person
And a groovy new skirt.
She is an untidy racket
And is like 'My Parents Are Aliens',
And a sticky treacle toffee.

**Laura McDonald  (11)**
**Barshare Primary School, Cumnock**


## Tomas Buffel

Tomas Buffel is glory blue
He's a bright summer's morning at Ibrox Park
He's a red sunset
He's a bright blue Ger's shirt
He's a fluffy blue sofa
He's a Scot's port
And a warm steak pie with gravy.

**Brendan Hay  (11)**
**Barshare Primary School, Cumnock**


## My Best Friend

Darren is as red as a lobster
He's as bright as a summer's day
On the beach he is tanned
He's hot and sunny
He's a pair of football boots
And a tidy desk
He's Scotsport
And a chocolate sticky pudding.

**William Robson  (11)**
**Barshare Primary School, Cumnock**

# My Gran

My gran is gold
She's a breezy summer evening
In a flowery back garden.
She's the clear blue sky,
She's a lovely flowery dress
And a warm, comfortable armchair.
She's 'Who Wants To Be A Millionaire?'
And a delicious apple turnover with cream.

**David Walker  (11)**
**Barshare Primary School, Cumnock**


# My Teacher

Mrs Burley is yellow
She's between summer and autumn
In a quiet classroom
She's a breezy day
She's a nightgown
On a comfy armchair
She's a millionaire
And a lemon meringue pie.

**Jessica Cameron  (10)**
**Barshare Primary School, Cumnock**


# My Brother

My brother is green
He's a warm sunny day
In a swimming pool
He's the hot sun
He's a football strip
And a warm bed
He's Setanta Sport
And a Spicy Curry Pot Noodle.

**Kieran Campbell  (11)**
**Barshare Primary School, Cumnock**

## My Brother

My brother is light blue
He is a cold, snowy, cloudy day
In Cumnock
He is snowy
He is trousers and a top
He is an old chair
He is 'The Addams Family'
And a cheesecake.

**Jay Keggans (10)**
**Barshare Primary School, Cumnock**


## Friend

Jessica is pink
She is summer.
In a beach
She is a sunny person.
She is a pair of jeans
She is a tidy desk
She is 'That's So Raven'
And a plate of ice cream.

**Rebecca Hodge (10)**
**Barshare Primary School, Cumnock**


## My Gran

My gran's soft pink
She's a summer garden
And a warm beach
She's a warm sunny day
She's a comfy white coat
And a warm soft couch
She's a 'Looney Toon'
And a small pot of sugar.

**Arfa Nasir (10)**
**Barshare Primary School, Cumnock**

# My Mum

My mum is a lovely bright pink
She is a lovely summer's day
On a beach with gold sand and clear water
She is a warm sunny day with a breeze
She is a beautiful nightgown and a lovely new TV
She is 'Coronation Street'
And a plate of nice, warm, sticky pudding.

**Ashleigh Dickie (10)**
**Barshare Primary School, Cumnock**


# All Over The World

I've always dreamed of going to France
a place where you can dance and prance
I've always dreamed of going to Australia
where their cricket team are failures
I've always dreamed of going to Italy
a place where you can get very tickly.

**Steven Hutchison (10)**
**Claypotts Castle Primary School, Dundee**


# I Like My Brother

I like my brother
he's never in trouble
he always reads his book
and he's always good
I like my brother
he always acts like a scarecrow
and is never bothered about anyone.
I like my brother
he acts innocent but he's not.

**Mariam Kassam (10)**
**Claypotts Castle Primary School, Dundee**

# Our First Day At The New School

All the royal blue running about with their friends
                                and younger brothers or sisters
Shiny light blue huts where some classes are
People speaking to their friends
People speaking while they reunite with their friends
Then the bell strikes nine and everybody gasps
I feel the fresh air and I feel anxious
Everybody is excited
On my first day at Claypotts Castle Primary School.

**Nadia Simpson (10)**
**Claypotts Castle Primary School, Dundee**


# My Dad

I like my dad because he's strong, kind
and he sorts out problems when they go wrong.
He drives a cool car to places very far.
He's very good at making tea for you,
I like my dad and he likes me.

**Roy Macaskill (10)**
**Claypotts Castle Primary School, Dundee**


# Frights

I love giving people a fright
Yesterday I hid behind the light
I jumped on my mum, she leapt in the air
And I ran up the stair
I hid under my bed
My mum shouted, 'You're going to be dead!'

**Louise Dunn (9)**
**Claypotts Castle Primary School, Dundee**

# New School

Bright, new, royal blue sweatshirts shining in the daylight
Children saying goodbye to their mums and dads
Running to play with their friends
The playground is like a deep blue sea
Everyone smiling and running about madly!
Teachers coming out because the old bell rings
All of the teachers saying hello to their new pupils
Children getting worried about what is going to happen
And who they are going to sit beside.

**Gemma Hutchison  (10)**
**Claypotts Castle Primary School, Dundee**


# Our First Day

Sadness
Missing my old school
Everybody running mad
Everybody going daft
Everything going bad
I was looking so sad
What better way to start the day?
Easy for some to say!

**Bradley Skelly  (11)**
**Claypotts Castle Primary School, Dundee**


# Water

W ater is a special thing
A nd helps to keep us clean
T ap water which we can drink
E ven helps us wash our jeans
R ight! Don't waste water.

**Jamie Lowrey  (10)**
**Claypotts Castle Primary School, Dundee**

# First Day At Claypotts Castle Primary School

*Noisy, noisy, bash, bash*
Lots of hilarity coming my way
Talk about our new school
Over four hundred smiles come towards the gates
Some children happy, unhappy and some cheery
I feel sad
I miss my old school
Happy I meet new friends
Here I am - the first ever Primary Seven
At Claypotts Castle Primary School.

**Rachel Cameron  (11)**
**Claypotts Castle Primary School, Dundee**


# Mr Crepsley

Mr Crepsley is ruby-red.
He is a creepy winter's night
In a  big, horrid castle.
He is a car wreck on the A90.
He is 'The Adams Family'
And is crab covered with vinegar.

**Gavin Lee Thomson  (10)**
**Claypotts Castle Primary School, Dundee**


# Dogs

I like dogs
The soft, cuddly, playful kind
The run-outside-to-lick me, to teach-it-tricks kind
To take it for a walk
I do like dogs.

**Keira Ann Duff  (10)**
**Claypotts Castle Primary School, Dundee**

# Our First Day At Claypotts Castle Primary

The playground like a deep blue sea
Unfamiliar faces all around me
Shiny new shoes shining in the sun
Lots of kids having fun
New teachers wandering around
Children having fun in the playground
Parents saying goodbye
But some of them want to cry
Everyone nervous, anxious and afraid
But we have to go to school to work and the teachers get paid!
All the teachers are coming - oh no I'm first!
For some reason I feel like I'm about to burst
Everyone's heart pumping scared to go inside
Some of them just want to hide
Children working hard on a hot summer's day
Concentrating in such a deep way.

**Natalie Smith (11)**
**Claypotts Castle Primary School, Dundee**


# Brand New School

Kids were running about the playground
Suddenly my heart started to pound
Blue sweatshirts with Douglas tartan ties
Most people I met were shy - no surprise
I looked at my new royal blue shirt
I looked at everyone else's - not one spot of dirt
People were bothered with their image - mostly hairdos
Then I looked at their feet, all shiny black shoes
People trying to be really cool
Why am I nervous? I'm part of
Claypotts Castle Primary School.

**Sam Gillan Whyte (11)**
**Claypotts Castle Primary School, Dundee**

# New School

Busy, busy playground
Full 'til it's like it's going to burst
Children hear the bell, run to line
Oh no, I'm first!
Teachers looking at the playground
Feeling like they're drowning in a deep blue sea
Teachers saying, 'Oh, hello, welcome to our school
I hope you enjoy being with me.'
Feeling nervous, feeling sad
This is the worst day I've ever had!
But then you get to know them
Always having laughs and cheers
Then you think, *why was I sad*?
*It feels like I've been here for years!*

**Tayler Anderson  (11)**
**Claypotts Castle Primary School, Dundee**


# First Day At Claypotts Castle

Everybody's heart was thumping
They were scared to go inside Claypotts Castle
Everyone just went to hide
One person shouted, 'School is cool!'
And everyone came out
We heard babies cry
Mums saying, 'Behave.'
And children just wanting to go inside
We also heard voices
Mrs McLaren came out
Everyone gasped but she said,
'Welcome to Claypotts Castle everyone.'
Everybody said, 'Hooray!'

**Hinna Kassam  (11)**
**Claypotts Castle Primary School, Dundee**

# First Day

It's a busy day at Claypotts Castle Primary
Mums and dads talking to each other
Young children running around
Buggies coming in and out of the playground
People playing football and jumping up and down and shouting
P1s crying for their mums and dads
Then the bell is ringing
All the children run to their lines.

**Duncan Gillon (11)**
**Claypotts Castle Primary School, Dundee**


# Kittens

I like kittens
The soft, fluffy, furry kind
The scratching kind.
I play with one
And feed it
I do like kittens!

**Nicola Forbes (9)**
**Claypotts Castle Primary School, Dundee**


# Christmas

Snow is falling,
Winter is calling,
Sound of sleigh bells,
Ring and ding,
Father Christmas is coming,
Carol singers humming,
Christmas time is here.

**Angela Scott (10)**
**Claypotts Castle Primary School, Dundee**

# First Day At Claypotts

On my first day, in my mind I saw a deep blue sea
And I felt I was drowning with all the royal blue
Big blue cabins to match our sweatshirts
A massive line of parents standing by the school wall
Primary 1's crying because they were leaving their mums
New head teacher standing at the gate, welcoming the parents
Wonderfully polished black school shoes
Bulging bags with gym kit, pencils and paper
Children laughing and playing in the sun
Older ones inspecting the cabins, the grass, the space.
*Rriinngg!*
That's the bell, time to go.

**Emma Burnett (10)**
**Claypotts Castle Primary School, Dundee**


# Autumn Leaves

Autumn is the time for falling leaves,
The orange, red and golden kind,
The beautiful kind,
They're not rustling much,
Or getting into trouble,
I do like autumn leaves.

**Taylor Smart (10)**
**Claypotts Castle Primary School, Dundee**


# Steve

Steve is a cheesy orange
He is a leafy autumn day
In a crunchy garden
He is a flying cup in the air
He is a 'Van Helsing'
And a bowl of blood.

**Rebecca Lindsay (10)**
**Claypotts Castle Primary School, Dundee**

# New School Day

My first day was scary
I looked in
It was like animals running wild in blue, grey and black
I walked inside the gate
Did not know who to play with
Mums talking
Children shouting
Talking about Claypotts Castle Primary School
I felt scared like I was about to go on a roller coaster
I wanted to know more people.

**Frankie Moran (11)**
**Claypotts Castle Primary School, Dundee**

# Mr Crepsley

Mr Crepsley is red and black
He is a freezing winter's day
In a creepy coven
He is an eating machine
He is 'Mona the Vampire'
And fat bacon with blood on it.

**Stewart Cowie (10)**
**Claypotts Castle Primary School, Dundee**

# Wolf Man

Wolf Man is fiery red.
He is a fierce summer's day
In a loud volcano.
He's a vicious dog.
He is 'Scary Movie 3'
And a bowl of very hot peppers.

**Iain Sandeman (10)**
**Claypotts Castle Primary School, Dundee**

# Our First Day

Bright blue sweatshirts like the ocean blue
I wondered what to do
Many children wearing blue
And toddlers, mums and dads too
Within the ocean blue
At the end of the day I felt royal blue
Mrs McLaren shouting, 'Welcome to Claypotts, you!'

**Drew Mill  (10)**
**Claypotts Castle Primary School, Dundee**


# Mr Crepsley

Mr Crepsley is a dark black.
He is a stormy, wet, rainy day
In a creepy, damp hotel.
He is a hole in the wall.
He is 'Scary Movie 3'
And a bowl of slimy worms.

**Caitlyn Mooney  (10)**
**Claypotts Castle Primary School, Dundee**


# Annie

Annie is shiny yellow.
She is a summery day
in a very hot desert.
She is a daisy.
She is 'The Parent Trap'.
She is a bowl of strawberries.

**Shannon Livingstone  (9)**
**Claypotts Castle Primary School, Dundee**

## Madam Octa

Madam Octa is deadly black.
She is a freezing cold winter
In a small spooky cage.
She is 'Eight-Legged Freaks'.
She eats dead flies.

**Christine Smith  (10)**
**Claypotts Castle Primary School, Dundee**


## Hans Hands

Hans Hands is light grey.
He is a hot summer's day
in a blazing desert.
He is a spinning tornado.
He is 'Scary Movie 1'
and a crispy chicken.

**Sam Dickson  (10)**
**Claypotts Castle Primary School, Dundee**


## Annie

Annie is lush pink.
She is a heart-melting summer's day
on a white sandy beach.
She is a shining star.
She is 'Angelina Ballerina'
and a bowl of Angel Delight.

**Caroline Milne  (10)**
**Claypotts Castle Primary School, Dundee**

## Annie

Annie is bright pink.
She is a scorching hot summer's day
in a brightly-coloured room.
She is a feathery ballet dress.
She is 'Babe'
and a cold ice lolly!

**Morven McGregor  (10)**
**Claypotts Castle Primary School, Dundee**


## Mr Crepsley

Mr Crepsley is dark red.
He is a freezing winter's day
in a creepy castle.
He's a big eating machine.
He is 'Most Haunted'.
He is ice cream with blood on it.

**Dale Grier  (10)**
**Claypotts Castle Primary School, Dundee**


## Madam Octa

Madam Octa is a dark, hairy black.
She is a cold winter's day
in a creepy, dark cellar.
She is 'Goosebumps'
and is a bowl of hot peppers!

**Allan McNicol  (10)**
**Claypotts Castle Primary School, Dundee**

# Annie

Annie is apple-red
She is a hot summer holiday
in a swimming pool.
She is the toy doll in the shop.
She is Lisa from 'The Simpsons'
and the ice cream running down an ice cream cone.

**Bobbie Sandeman  (9)**
**Claypotts Castle Primary School, Dundee**


# Madam Octa

Madam Octa is dark, dark black.
She is a dull winter's night
in a dark hole in your house.
She is a horrible, hairy creature!
She is 'Eight-Legged Freaks'
and a bowl of horrible stovies.

**Chloe Anderson  (10)**
**Claypotts Castle Primary School, Dundee**


# Steve

Steve is a very light pink.
He is a bright, hot, summery spring
in a bonny bedroom.
He is a jack-in-the-box.
He is 'Cat in the Hat'
and a yummy KFC.

**Lori Allan  (9)**
**Claypotts Castle Primary School, Dundee**

# Blue Hoods

Blue Hoods are mysterious black.
They are a gruesome winter's day
in a cellar taking care of the freaks!
They are the claws of a tiger
striking an antelope.
They are 'Most Haunted'.
They are burnt chips with salad.

**Hannah Fisher  (9)**
**Claypotts Castle Primary School, Dundee**


# Hans Hands

Hans Hands is a cold black.
He is a rainy winter's night
in an abandoned car.
He is a Formula 1 Aston Martin.
He is 'Most Haunted'
and a snail sandwich.

**Andrew Cowie  (10)**
**Claypotts Castle Primary School, Dundee**


# Madam Octa

Madam Octa is deadly black!
She is a freezing cold winter
in a small spooky cage.
She is a metal flute.
She is 'Eight-Legged Freaks'
and lots of dead flies.

**Danielle Crawford  (9)**
**Claypotts Castle Primary School, Dundee**

# Deep Blue School

Our first day at Claypotts Castle Primary School
I was so nervous and I felt like I was drowning in an ocean
                                            of royal blue
I felt like I did not know one person, the school was so packed.
I could hear lots of people shouting
And the bell
And my new teacher.

**Ryan Webster  (11)**
**Claypotts Castle Primary School, Dundee**


# Snake Boy

Snake Boy is slimy black.
He is an ugly autumn
in a pile of wet leaves.
He's the slime off a slug.
He is 'The Jungle Book'
and a bowl of burnt carrots.

**Courtney Roache  (10)**
**Claypotts Castle Primary School, Dundee**


# Rhamus Twobellies

Rhamus Twobellies is greasy yellow.
He is a rainy autumn day
in a yummy chip shop.
He is an enormous junkyard.
He is 'Ready, Steady, Cook'
and a McChicken value meal.

**Rachael Lyall  (10)**
**Claypotts Castle Primary School, Dundee**

## Mr Crepsley

Mr Crepsley is dark black and red.
He is a chilly winter's night in a haunted castle.
He is a black bat.
He is 'Van Helsing' and a bowl of slimy, slippery squid.

**Dyllon Jeffrey (10)**
**Claypotts Castle Primary School, Dundee**

## Mr Crepsley

Mr Crepsley is ghastly grey.
He is a frosty, dark winter's night
in a dark cellar.
He is saliva from a bear's mouth.
He is 'The Exorcist'
and a bowl of tomatoes with custard.

**Shaun Hendry (10)**
**Claypotts Castle Primary School, Dundee**

## Madam Octa

Madam Octa is dark black.
She is a cold day
in a freezing cellar.
She is a smelly stray dog.
She is 'Freddy vs Jason'
and a bowl of slimy eels!

**Javed Din (9)**
**Claypotts Castle Primary School, Dundee**

# New School

*Dring-dring!*
There goes my alarm clock
Rush out of bed
Run to the living room
See Mum with breakfast on the table
Eat my breakfast
Try not to spill milk down my PJs
Get washed and dressed
Get coat and bag and run out the door
                    without saying bye to Mum
And off I go to school
See my friends
Run over to them
Say, 'What class are you in?'
Lots of new faces
We all get to know each other
The day goes fast
*Ring ring!*
We all line up
Make it safely out of school
*Awww!*
Another hard day tomorrow.

**Kiera Cartmill (11)**
**Claypotts Castle Primary School, Dundee**

# Fog On Guard

Walking along a sandy beach,
The fog, he's rolling in,
He wraps his thick black arms round me,
My body, white and thin.

My eyes are weak,
He pulls my senses out of me,
My hearing is all muffled,
Will my senses ever be free?

When is the sun coming?
When shall the fog go?
How will I ever get home?
How should anyone know?

There is a sun warrior,
Breaking through the fog walls,
He turns round to see,
But dies and then he falls!

Now I can hear,
Now I can see,
But, most importantly,
All of me is free!

**Hannah Burt  (9)**
**Cults Primary School, Cults**

# Fog And I

Fog was everywhere in the town of Aberdeen,
It followed me into the shops and out again,
My mum looked just like a great big blob,
I tried to run away from it but it wouldn't go.

I caught the next express train that took me to Dundee
But I forgot to get off and it took me back to Aberdeen,
I ran all the way home but I couldn't find my house,
Soon, I did find my house and it was very big,
I bumped into the wall because I couldn't see a thing,
It followed me into the house, it wouldn't go away.

It was there the next day and it followed me to school,
At break it ate my snack for me and that was very cruel,
I felt some water on my face and a voice saying,
'Wake up and open your eyes, it's time for school, it's a lovely
                                                    foggy day.'
I must have been dreaming into the future.

**Tegan Seivwright (9)**
**Cults Primary School, Cults**


# Thick Fog

Thick fog covering the ground
Making my head spin round and round
So thick the fog, I cannot see
Not a soul can even see me
The sound of traffic comes to my ears
My face so wet, it is like tears
I can hear people and they can hear me
But the people are one thing I cannot see
The fog so thick, the planes are delayed
New schedules are being made
All the while I start to wonder
Will I get home or go yonder?

**Fiona Thompson (10)**
**Cults Primary School, Cults**

# The Fog

The world has been covered in a pale white cloth,
I feel like a blind man,
The cars are huge, mechanical monsters racing past,
It is night and there is no breeze,
Somebody has smothered me in a milky sheet,
I am choking in this horrible alternative to the world.

There are bats flying overhead,
It feels like they are clawing my hair,
I'm screaming but a pearl gag is stopping me,
I need to find home,
But I don't know where to turn to . . .

This milky world should be gone
Let me go, leave me alone!

**Lucy Smith  (10)**
**Cults Primary School, Cults**


# Mysterious, Spooky Fog

The rain falls and fog begins
It is mysterious and spooky
It rushes past me like a zooming racing car
It swishes, turns, twists, tumbles and glides
Up and down, side to side it goes
Hours and hours it stays, never makes a sound
The sound is muffled and your eyesight is blurred
Making no noise, it disappears; the sun comes out
I see it's gone, but I know it will return.

**Eilidh Scott  (10)**
**Cults Primary School, Cults**

# Foggy Danger!

Fog is a mist,
Sometimes thick, sometimes thin,
Fog can cause casualties if very thick,
We need to get out of the fog, quick! Quick!

Can you hear that little cry
As we pass the little boy by?
Should we help him,
Or should we stay safe?
What should we do?
Fog is a really big clue!

Fog is *danger!*
Don't go near it,
Fog can happen any time, any place,
It really is a race!
Who will win - fog and mist
Or the humans?

Cars go *bash!*
When they *crash!*

I try to scream
Because of this horrible, scary scene!

'Help! Help!' I want to go
But I can't!
I can't see, I can't touch anything!
                              *'Help!'*

**Eve Norris  (9)**
**Cults Primary School, Cults**

# Fog

All I can see is the colour of the sky over the heavy mist
It comes right up to me
I think it's my friend but is it my enemy?
It comes up to hug me as if I'm a teddy bear
But then it disappears once again with no warning at all
It covers me like a blanket over my eyes and ears.

Everything from afar seems to be so near
Everything so near becomes so far
Fog will come and blind you
And leave you in dismay.

**Trishna Raj  (10)**
**Cults Primary School, Cults**


# Fog

Thick fog covering the ground,
So quiet and dark,
I cannot see anything or anyone,
And they can't see me,
It's really spooky,
People are banging into things,
No lights in the neighbourhood,
I just wish the fog would go away,
It's 8 o'clock in the morning,
It is as dark as a big black hole,
I am holding my mum's hand tight,
I am really, really, really scared.

**Atlanta Taylor Hearns  (9)**
**Cults Primary School, Cults**

# The Fruits Of The Harvest

Down by the burn I pick
Big green pears and red apples,
I will make a pudding from them tonight.

Into the meadow I go, to get
Big juicy brambles and raspberries,
I fill a punnet of each and share with my friends.

Up the hill I climb to the farm,
Where I am greeted by the farm dogs,
They make me drop my berries but collect them for me again.

Into the house I go and Mum makes a cake
With all the food I brought in,
It was a very nice cake indeed.

**Ailsa Goldie (10)**
**Drumbowie Primary School, Falkirk**


# Harvest Time

I'm always busy,
I run about,
I eat anything,
I am a . . . ?

I'm always thirsty,
But I like the sun,
I am always being bashed,
I am the . . . ?

I can be any size,
I don't have fur,
I can be eaten,
I am a . . . ?

**Hayley Walker (10)**
**Drumbowie Primary School, Falkirk**

# Harvest

Under the sea
the fish are swimming away
as the fishermen try to catch them.

Below the sun
the wheat is being cut
by the farmer.

Near the farm
the crops are growing
to feed us before the winter comes.

Against the farm's fence
the cows are mooing
and eating the grass.

In the meadow
the combine harvester
is cutting the grain.

Behind the tree
the farm animals
are working for harvest.

**Abbie McLean  (9)**
**Drumbowie Primary School, Falkirk**


# The Harvest Birds Calling

The harvest birds are calling, calling, calling
And Farmer Jock saw the leaves falling,

                    falling,

                          falling.

He said goodbye to the harvest birds, 'Goodbye, goodbye, goodbye.
I don't want you to leave,' he said with a sigh, sigh, sigh.

**Eilidh Park  (7)**
**Drumbowie Primary School, Falkirk**

# Harvest Is The Time Of Year When . . .

Harvest
is the
time of year
when
farmers cut
the crops and
fishermen
are busy
preparing
the fish
for the shops.
The divers
are
very busy
collecting
gas and oil
that has
been brought
to us
through many
dangerous toils.
Harvest
is
the time
of year when
everyone
is happy
and we have
lots
of food
to eat
throughout
the
year.

**Hannah Crawford  (8)**
**Drumbowie Primary School, Falkirk**

# Autumn Harvest

The yellow leaves are falling,
>> falling
>>> falling

But first they go brown,
Then they go orange.
The autumn leaves are falling,
>> falling,
>>> falling.

**Kelly Montgomery  (7)**
**Drumbowie Primary School, Falkirk**


# Please Pick Me!

How long till I'm picked?
My eyes beg silently
I want to go home
How could my mum do this to me?
Please somebody,
*Please, pick me!*

Tears are welling up in my eyes
I blink them away
All I want is my mum
To give me a hug
And say, 'Everything will be OK.'
Please somebody,
*Please pick me!*

There's a lump in my throat
And it won't go away.
All the pretty ones are picked
How come I'm still here?
Mum always said
I was her little angel
Please somebody,
*Please pick me!*

**Rhea Shearer  (11)**
**Dunecht School, Westhill**

# When Will I Be Picked?

Who will pick me?
I am cold
There's a lump in my throat
That won't go away
Please pick me!
My eyes are welling up
My face is hot and flushed
How long will it take?

One by one
Children are chosen
But why not me?
I will be posh,
Clean, strong,
I bend down to tie my shoe,
Pretty please!
Who will pick me?

**Caroline Sim  (10)**
**Dunecht School, Westhill**


# Waiting To Be Picked

Who will pick me?
There's a lump in my throat
That won't go away
It's making it hard to swallow
Knees are wobbling
When will I be picked?
I blink back the tears
My chin starts to quiver
Looking up through bleary eyes at the strangers
I bite my lip to stop it
My eyes well up with tears
One lonely tear slides out
Rubbing my homesick tummy
What do I have to do to get picked?

**Calum Rae  (10)**
**Dunecht School, Westhill**

# Will I Get Picked?

Standing at the station
Cringing with embarrassment
At my dirty shoes
Pull up my wrinkled socks
Trying to be brave

Eyes welling up
There's a lump in my throat
And it won't go away
I try to blink back the tears
Worrying who will pick me up

Knees are wobbling
Trying hard to stop them
Shiver with dread
Wanting a hug, feeling so lonely
I want to go home
Finally . . .
Someone's picked *me!*

**Amber Dawson  (11)**
**Dunecht School, Westhill**

# Evacuation

I hope I'll be picked
I feel like I'm going to faint
Feeling so nervous
I feel I want to cry
I hope I won't be last
There's a knot in my tummy
Thinking about Mum
All alone back in town
I hope she's fine
My stomach feels ripped open
Feeling so homesick
I want to go home
Back to my mum.

**Alan McCombie  (11)**
**Dunecht School, Westhill**

# An Evacuee's Journey

As I walk into the train
I look at my mum feeling the pain
My eyes begin to swell
Mum's waving tearfully
I wave back, trying to be brave
With a tear in my eye.

The train's stopped
Where am I?
I look around nervously
The teacher leads us to a street
Then lots of strangers come
I wonder who will be my new mum.

I start shuffling my feet
I try blinking my tears away
I want to run home
There goes Violet
Now James.

There is someone staring at me
Well, someone *was* staring at me
Why is nobody picking me?

**Hayley O'Brien  (10)**
**Dunecht School, Westhill**

# Evacuation

*(From a teacher's eye)*

'Hurry Daisy, get off,
You too, Jimmy,
They're waiting,
Quickly, the train's starting,
I don't care about the brown bag,
Just get off.'

There go Eddie, Marvin and Daisy,
All trying to be brave,
The twins, George and Violet, only five left,
Who will be next?

Here comes a farmer, takes Jimmy and Charles,
Ah, there goes Betty with tears in her eyes,
Gosh, only Ruby and her brother Ronald,
No one is coming,
What will happen to them?

As well as them,
There is me.
Only a teacher,
Where will I go?

**Caitlin Drummond  (10)**
**Dunecht School, Westhill**

# My Evacuation

I've been sent away
to the countryside far away,
away from town,
it's quiet all around,
I'm feeling homesick,
when will I be picked?

I'm stopping my tears
from falling down my cheek,
as I look at the ground
and shuffle my feet.
My eyes cloud up
and it's hard to see
and next thing I know
is that someone's picked me!

I'm led to a place
that I presume
is meant to be my own bedroom!
It's really dusty and really not nice
there are spiders and cobwebs
and scampering mice!

I hate it here!
I want to leave!
I'm really sad,
right to the bone,
I want to leave!
Just let me go home.

**Kenneth MacBeath  (10)**
**Dunecht School, Westhill**

# Waiting To Be Picked

Sitting waiting.
Waiting to get there.
How long will it take?
My chin starts to quiver,
Like it's never done before!
Worrying about Mum,
What is going to happen?

We climb out of the train,
One by one.
My heart has been ripped out,
And replaced with nothing.
Slowly the line gets shorter and shorter,
As everyone is picked!

Now it's just me and my brother,
Looking at the ground, shuffling our feet
And begging to be picked.
Is it? Could it be? Yes, I have been picked!
But my brother is still standing there.
What will Mum say?

**Kerryn McRae  (10)**
**Dunecht School, Westhill**


# A Child's View

As the children walk away
Their mothers are waving them away.
Can't I get my own way?
As I lie in a strange bed
I think, *is Mum dead*?
People laugh at me for being so strange
They say, 'She is a town kid,' but I always remember,
'Chin up,' the last words my mum said
Before I was torn away from my loved ones.

**Hannah Johnston  (10)**
**Dunecht School, Westhill**

# Waiting To Be Chosen

Shoulders slump,
feet go clump,
waiting to be chosen.

Face goes cringe,
trying to sort my hair and fringe,
waiting to be chosen.

My face is hot and flushed.
Oh why can't the war be rushed?
Waiting to be chosen.

I blink back tears,
and try not to show that I fear,
waiting to be chosen.

I want to go home!
I'm feeling so alone,
waiting to be chosen.

Oh, when will I be chosen?

**Kyla Hislop (10)**
**Dunecht School, Westhill**


# When Will I Be Picked?

Standing at the station,
With no concentration,
Waiting to be picked,
Hope it's no one strict!

Knees are wobbling, weak with exhaustion,
Thinking, *when will I be picked*?
Face is hot and flushed,
Hope my hair is brushed!

I'm being picked . . . but . . .
*Oh no! It's someone strict!*

**Finlay McPherson (9)**
**Dunecht School, Westhill**

# Evacuated

Standing waiting,
With a lump in my throat.
It's hard to swallow,
My throat feels hollow,
It won't go away,
It has to stay!
Can it just go away?

Standing waiting,
Is it ten o'clock?
When will I be picked?
My eyes are begging silently,
I'm blinking back the fear!

Standing waiting,
Can't I be picked?
For once I'm unlucky!
The lump's gone deeper,
It really is a shock,
No one wants me!
Suddenly the keeper
Comes up to me,
'Are you lost?'
*'No!* I want to be free!
Can't someone just pick me?'

**Monique Hendy  (9)**
**Dunecht School, Westhill**

# Waiting To Be Picked

Standing nervously
Waiting, waiting
When will I get picked?
Brushing down my hair
Tidying up my shirt
Waiting to get picked.

What's wrong with me?
Blinking away my tears
All the children getting picked
Except me!
A lump in my throat
Feel like I am going to be sick
I want to go home!
I want to go home!

Shuffling my feet
Itching my head
Trying to smile
For when will someone pick me?

**Joanna Cook  (10)**
**Dunecht School, Westhill**

# When Will I Be Picked?

Who will pick me?
There's a lump in my throat
Knees are wobbling
When will I be picked?

My chin starts to quiver
I blink back the tears
My shoulders slump
When will I be picked?

I don't like it here
The tears are stinging my eyes
I'm trying to look smarter but
When will I be picked?

I want to go home!
One lonely tear slides out
Trying to be brave
When will I be picked?

**Scott Campbell (10)**
**Dunecht School, Westhill**

# Waiting, Waiting, Waiting

Close as I can
Sticking to my friends
Trying to be brave. Waiting, waiting, waiting
When will I be picked?

Why has Mum done this to me
Sending me away
To a different, strange place?
My eyes beg silently
'Please someone, please pick me.'
But I'm waiting, waiting, waiting
And no one's picking me.

My spine tingles with a cold sweat
Blushing with embarrassment.
Eyes are stinging with tears
Trying hard to look smart
But I'm still waiting, waiting, waiting . . .

And no one's picking me.

**Daniel Wilson  (8)**
**Dunecht School, Westhill**

# Evacuation

*Where are we?* I thought
my eyes crackling at the countryside.
What are those fluffy things
which I haven't seen before?
'Look, apples are growing on trees
I can't believe my eyes.'
Where are we?

Standing in the hall
shivering with dread
who will pick me?
My eyes are stinging with tears
I dread being picked last.
A farmer walks in without seeing the boys,
'I don't want girls,' he says
'I want boys,' he says, 'an three o' them!'
He spots us.
'Well, there ain't three of ye
but I'll take 'em.'
Phew! We've been picked.

**Stephen Hugh Will  (8)**
**Dunecht School, Westhill**

# I Am Waiting, I Am Waiting

I am waiting
I am waiting
For the train.
Finally it comes
I shall be brave.
Violet my friend
Is shivering with dread
Tommy's eyes are stinging
With lonely tears.

Climbing onto the train
Off we go,
Waving to my family
I've got a lump in my throat
One sad tear slides out
Hoping no one sees it.
I keep gulping but the lump won't go
Why has Mum done this to me?

I am waiting
I am waiting
Waiting to be picked.
Tommy is first
Violet is second
Who will pick me?
Cringing with embarrassment
No one picks me!

**Skye Dawson  (9)**
**Dunecht School, Westhill**

# Waiting, Waiting, Waiting To Be Chosen

I clutch onto my younger brother, Charlie,
I have an urge to cry.
I can't 'cause
Charlie will start crying.

I pace back and forth
Back and forth
But I stop
Start to think
*I am not leaving*
*Without Charlie*
*Never, ever, ever!*

Someone comes along
Wants only me
'No I am not going
Without Charlie!'
'I respect that,
I'll take you both.'
I was waiting, waiting, waiting,
Now we've been picked.

**Cameron Brownie  (9)**
**Dunecht School, Westhill**

# Being Evacuated

The train's started
Waiting for an everlasting journey
With everlasting thoughts,
*Is Mum dead?*
*What about my friends?*
Here we are, the countryside,
Coming off the train, lining up,
I've got butterflies in my stomach
In a cold sweat,
One by one,
Children are picked
By wealthy or poor people.
There goes Betty,
She's not ready.
Now it's only *me!*

**Philip Oakes  (9)**
**Dunecht School, Westhill**


# My Friend

She is called
Laura Ann.
She has a voice
Like a nightingale.
Her ears are pierced.
She has blonde hair.
She wears red trousers
And a red jumper.

She wears
White trainers.
She has a Jesus necklace.
The cross is gold
And Jesus is silver.
She is scared
Of animals.

**Davie Campbell  (9)**
**Easdale Primary School, Oban**

# Seasons

Spring is the season when lambs are born and flowers grow.
Spring has a nice smell and you feel lovely and special.
In spring you look forward to another year.

Summer is hot and very nice.
I feel like diving in the sea and shouting, 'I'm free!'
And I do it sometimes.
I love summer!

In autumn the leaves fall off the trees.
I love trailing through the leaves with my feet,
And when I have to say goodbye to autumn I say hello to winter.

In winter snow usually falls and I see children sledging along
And the sledge makes tracks in the ground,
When I say goodbye to winter I look forward to another year.

**Gillian MacKechnie (9)**
**Easdale Primary School, Oban**

# My Friend Megan

My friend Megan is a really good friend.
I like the way she laughs or giggles.
It's like a ray of sunshine on a dark grey day.

She has blonde highlights in her brown feathered locks.
She loves horses and is a great rider.

She has pierced ears and a mobile phone.
She's allowed to go to Oban all on her own.

She really likes maths and plays the flute.
When she does, it sounds like a toot.

She's my friend and I love her to bits.
I couldn't live without her that's just it.

**Jenny Case (9)**
**Easdale Primary School, Oban**

# Seasons

Spring is when the calves are born
and the flowers begin to grow.
Spring is when the leaves unfold
on the tallest trees in the meadow.
Spring is when the birds set camp
and the grass is very damp.

In the summer the birds will sing
and the sun is very hot.
In the summer the sea is warm
and I go swimming a lot.
I hate it when the sand gets in-between your toes
you rub it with a towel but it never really goes.

Autumn comes with shorter days
and the spookiest Hallowe'en.
Autumn comes with falling leaves
and the fields are no longer green.
Autumn brings us Bonfire Night
when fireworks are set alight.

Winter brings us the whitest snow
and a blazing fire.
Icy mornings, frozen feet,
but I don't like days that just bring sleet.
Christmas is the best of all
God bless us, one and all.

**Sam Nichols  (10)**
**Easdale Primary School, Oban**

# Seasons

*Spring*    I like spring, never won't
It has a heart that never dies and never will.
I give it pleasure, I give it pride
But I have spring last on my list.

*Summer*    Summer is bright, it's like a kite
That never comes down.
It flies high
Summer always flies away.
I couldn't live without it.

*Autumn*    Autumn is fine, it's like a vine
That doesn't grow very well.
It is kind but very strong.

Winter    It is my favourite season
I can't live without snow.
The horses have their coats on
The mice are quiet.
When I say goodbye to winter
I say hello to spring again.

I love the seasons.

**Rebekah Freya Stephenson (9)**
**Easdale Primary School, Oban**

# Seasons

Spring, I love you
You are so beautiful and quiet
You are the best season
The birds sing
The days get longer
Everything is green.

Summer is hot,
Summer is sunny, the days are the longest
I can swim in the sea and make sandcastles
The weather is beautiful and bright
I like this season
Because summer is wonderful.

The houses and trees are wet
The leaves are red, yellow and brown
And they fall softly to the ground
The weather is cloudy and rainy
I like autumn because
There are lots of fruits.

It's winter, it's night
It's snowy and white
It's a beautiful winter
It's a wonderful year
Christmas is coming
All the children are here.

**Hannah Croucher  (10)**
**Easdale Primary School, Oban**

# The Seasons

*Summer*
Summertime, the swallows sing
Summertime, farmers bale the hay
Summertime, fishermen fish on the bay
And bees collect the honey.

*Autumn*
In autumn leaves fall off the trees
It's hibernation time for the bees
Bulbs are planted in the soil
Fishing lines are in a coil
And ploughs are used to turn the soil.

*Winter*
Wintertime, children play in the snow
Wintertime, the temperature is low
Snowballs are thrown
Christmas trumpets are blown
And turkeys groan.

*Spring*
Flowers in the garden are blooming
Choirs in the street are singing
Gardeners are getting rid of weeds
While farmers sow their seeds
And tadpoles grow amongst the reeds.

**Gordon Phillips  (10)**
**Easdale Primary School, Oban**

# Seasons

There are four seasons,
Spring, summer, autumn, winter.
Spring, I see the calves frolicking in the fields
Summer, I see the sun coming out
Autumn, I see the leaves falling from the trees
And winter I see the snowflakes falling from the sky.

There are four seasons,
Spring, summer, autumn, winter.
Spring, I smell the fresh air
Summer, I smell the flowers
Autumn, I smell the orange and brown leaves
And winter I smell the chimney smoke.

There are four seasons
Spring, summer, autumn, winter
Spring, I hear the lambs baaing
Summer, I hear the birds singing
Autumn, I hear the brown leaves scrunching
And winter, I hear myself sniffing in the cold.

There are four seasons,
Spring, summer, autumn, winter
Spring, I touch the baby lambs
Summer, I touch the daffodils
Autumn, I touch the bare trees
And winter I touch the cold white snowflakes.

There are four seasons
Spring, summer, autumn, winter
Spring, I taste the bees' honey
Summer, I taste the warm air
Autumn, I taste the sweet brambles
And winter, I taste the snowflakes.

**Megan Gilroy (11)**
**Easdale Primary School, Oban**

## I Like Bonny

Bonny is a hero
When I am sad
Bonny comes to save me
But when I'm better
She goes to play
With her ball and wren
She is so fast
When we go on a walk
She pulls me up the biggest hills
When I go on Ruffy
Joe and my dad and Bonny run with me.

She jumps up at my mum
It makes me and Joe want to do it.

**Holly Wesley  (8)**
**Easdale Primary School, Oban**


## World War I

The enemy is coming, hide!
Run as fast as we can
they are shooting at us.
Here comes the Spitfire
*Bang! Argh!*
I will get you.

I can hear footsteps of the enemy
coming towards me
and the rat-a-tat of the machine guns.

The blood covers all the battlefield.

The enemy is chasing me
they are catching up with me
they have caught me!

**Daryl Coutts  (10)**
**Eastbank Primary School, Shettleston**

# My Rabbit

My rabbit always jumps around
he always likes to hop
when my mum first bought him
he chewed her nice red top.

My rabbit's really furry
and he always makes me laugh
when I was eating chicken curry
he hopped into my bath.

My rabbit's really weird
he climbs up and down the stairs
when I was lying down yesterday
he was sniffing at my hair.

So there you have it,
        that's my rabbit!

**Jaye Brownlie  (11)**
**Eastbank Primary School, Shettleston**


# My First Sports Day

It's my first day of sports day
I don't know where to go
All the children running about
Like animals in the zoo.

The teacher tells me where to go
Suddenly I stub my toe
I'm running around like a crazy chicken
Then there is my grandma sitting knitting.

My mum and dad watching me
Drinking a little cup of tea
I think I really need a pee
Then I see a little cute bee.

**Dale Matthews  (11)**
**Eastbank Primary School, Shettleston**

# My First Day Of Primary 1

I had to listen and pay attention
and I had to know what to do
I was shy and nervous starting school
I heard people talking and playing games
so I wanted to join in because I was bored
so they said, 'Yes, okay.'

But when I joined in there was a problem
a boy was moaning and so selfish
he always wanted his own way
and he wouldn't sit on the set
he was really getting on my nerves
because he always liked to stand up.

When the bell rang, I went outside for playtime
I had crisps and juice and it was fun
but it was really cold outside
then a few minutes later we went back inside
and we did some work.

After that and more games
we came out and then it was lunchtime
so I ate my lunch and after that I had to go home.

**Natalie Colvin (11)**
**Eastbank Primary School, Shettleston**


# The Catch

I saw the glittering blue sea turn into crimson red,
as the spear went into the black and white killer whale's back.

I could hear the squeaky, screaming cries of the killer whale,
which made most of the glass cabin windows crack.

I could smell the sweat, which was disgusting, from all the men
as they were pulling out the spear from the whale.

The feeling of the cold, squidgy, slippery wetness of the killer
whale's tail gave me a shivery feeling down my back.

**Tyler McNeill (10)**
**Eastbank Primary School, Shettleston**

# The Japanese War

I still remember the destructive six years during the Japanese war.
Every day you could hear the bombs and the machine guns.
Everywhere you looked all you could see were bodies
                                                    covered in blood.
You could smell the ash and fire in the air.
Those six years were the hardest of my life.

I still remember the smoky feeling of the fire extinguisher and the
sound of the alarms going *brrng!* The screams and all of the horrible
                                        ice creams on the pavement.
Even small kids at the age of three were captured.

I still remember the planes' engines coming over to Pearl Harbour.
I still remember the cries of the innocent people, crying for their lives.
I still remember hearing the bombs falling on top of Hiroshima,
People singing and crying.

**Darren Currie  (11)**
**Eastbank Primary School, Shettleston**


# My First Day At School

My first day at school was very cool.
I felt bad when I left my dad.
I met a new friend called Sean.
He had never seen a prawn.

He cried and cried then he came with me.
I liked the teacher and she liked me,
But she was old and had a bad cold.

Sean hated the teacher so he acted cheekily to her,
And she got angry so she put him in the corner.
He said, 'Sorry,' and he came to play.
That was a cool day.

**Nathan Spencer  (10)**
**Eastbank Primary School, Shettleston**

# Night-Time

At night I can't wait to go to bed,
Just can't wait to snuggle up to my ted.
The moon and stars are very bright,
But the one thing is they only come out at night.

Before I go to bed I brush my teeth,
Then I say goodnight to my Uncle Keith.
I turn on the TV, it is very boring,
All I can hear is my big brother snoring.

Finally I get to sleep,
In the morning I have to tidy my toys, which are in a heap.
When I wake up, I can see,
My mum bringing in my hot tea.

**Erin Lilley  (10)**
**Eastbank Primary School, Shettleston**


# When I Wake Up

When I wake up in the morning,
I brush my hair for a while.
When I wake up in the morning,
I look in the mirror and smile.

In the morning my little sister is a pest,
Whenever I go to get dressed.
Even if she is a pest,
I still love her, she is the best.

When I give her my ball,
She doesn't annoy me at all.
She tries to play in the hall,
But it is too small.

She starts to cry,
And pulls my tie.
Then I wave bye-bye.

**Hayley Grant  (10)**
**Eastbank Primary School, Shettleston**

# The Hunt

The crimson red sea was like a strawberry mousse
sailing up and down in the fierce waves.
A whale as big as a school getting struck
by the sharpest spear you could think of.

The cry of the whale was like a deafening bomb
in my ears, so loud I could scream.
I could hear the oarsmen huffing and puffing
from the fast journey we'd just had.

I could taste the sandy, salty water
blowing on my ice-cold lips.
The fear was so terrific and terrifying
I could taste it.

Sweat is a vile, repulsive smell
which I smelt off the oarsmen.
I could smell the whale's blood
which wasn't very nice either.

I could feel the cold, gusting wind
whistling in my ears.
I felt the whale's smooth back
when it popped up to say, *'Hello!'*

**Lewis King (11)**
**Eastbank Primary School, Shettleston**

# Inside The Mind Of Billy!

Inside the mind of Billy was . . .
an angry anxious ant
a badly behaved dog
a cruel cat
a dashing dog
an elderly elephant
a frantic frog
a hairy, hungry hamster
an intelligent, ignorant imp
a joyful, jumping jellybean
a kicking kangaroo
a laughing lamb
a mad mango
a nasty, negative nit
an orange octopus
a purple penguin
a quiet quail
a raging rhino
a sad snake
a tired tiger
an untidy unicorn
a vast van
a wicked witch
a yelling, yelping yo-yo
and a zipping zebra inside the mind of Billy!

**David James Hendry (10)**
**Eastbank Primary School, Shettleston**

# My Old Cats

I sure miss my rats
No, I'm only kidding, they were cats
One was called Cheeky
And one was called Sly.

They were strange
And really freaky
They ate apples and pears
And their own cat hair
Cheeky was bad
And Sly was mad.

But what could I do?
Even though they smelt
I loved my cats so much!
I thought it could last
Until I was eight
Then my mum met her mate
My mum gave them away
To her friend called Evil May!

**Aimee Munro  (10)**
**Eastbank Primary School, Shettleston**


# Hunted

I see a boat not far ahead
Must remember what Mother said
I have to move quick and fast
Before the humans take a sharp, clean blast
No spear is going to go through me
For I am a predator of the sea.

**Gillian Ross  (11)**
**Eastbank Primary School, Shettleston**

# My Frenzied Family

My frenzied mum, she cleans a lot.
Then she cooks dinner in a giant pot.
Her hair's all frizzy and her make-up's a mess
I have a nickname for her, it's Frenzied Tess.

My frenzied dad, he moans a lot,
He says, 'Eat some fruit or it will rot!'
I always do it, he's such a pest
I wish he would just take a rest.

My frenzied cat, he eats a lot,
He likes tuna and eggs boiled in a pot.
My crazy cat, he sleeps loads
He makes my mum want to explode!

**Courtney Leigh Williamson  (11)**
**Eastbank Primary School, Shettleston**


# Stars

High above our heads,
Shimmering, sparkling, twinkling,
The north and south star shine.

What a dream if they could be mine,
Staring at them sparkle.
Oh, how I wish they weren't so far.
I wish I could touch a magic star.

Silver, sparkly and colourful to the eye,
Like a rainbow in the sky.
They look beautiful in the sky.
I wonder how they magically shine.

**Nichola Mulheron  (11)**
**Eastbank Primary School, Shettleston**

# Under The Sea

Under the sea what do I see?
A fish coming out from nowhere.
I see a jellyfish coming towards me,
I see the sharks coming closer and closer,
I see a flatfish under me.

I hear a dolphin,
I hear crabs clipping their claws,
I hear the noise above,
I can hear the waves.

I can feel the fish,
I can feel the flatfish,
I can feel the waves,
I feel the tip of a shark's tail.

**Jade Freeman  (10)**
**Eastbank Primary School, Shettleston**


# Dancing

Twirling, dancing around the room
Landing softly without a boom
A little pink tutu around my waist
Shimmering sparkles over my face
Majorette stick twirling in my hand
Marching to the beat of the loud brass band.

Sliding over the slippery floor
Making my way towards the door
It's time to take my stance
So I'll finish my dance
With a little girlie pose.

**Emily Meechan  (11)**
**Eastbank Primary School, Shettleston**

# The Pet Shop

Which pet to pick,
I really don't know,
All so cute and cuddly,
I just don't know.

What about a hamster?
What about a rabbit?
What about a bird?
So many to choose from,
I just don't know.

Hamsters just sleep,
Rabbits just eat,
Cats just purr,
Dogs just bark,
I just don't know,
Which pet to pick.

**Danielle Elizabith Alexander (10)**
**Eastbank Primary School, Shettleston**


# The Storm

Wind howling around my ears
Can't move, struck with fear
Thunder crackling overhead
Oh, how I wish I was in bed!

Rain pounding down on me
Almost hit by a falling tree
I'm lying down in the grass
Oh, how I wish this storm would pass!

My world is spinning round and round
I'm pinned into the muddy ground
Then the sun starts to shine
But now I've lost all that's mine.

**Jade Stirling (10)**
**Eastbank Primary School, Shettleston**

# In The New Town

In the new town there are . . .

Animals acting atrocious, answering, awkward aliens,
Blubbering babies being bullied by bossy boys,
Clever cooks carrying clean cutlery crazily,
Destructive dunces dancing dizzily,
Erupting enemies eating enormous eggs,
Furious French fiends fibbing fluently in French,
Grotty grannies giggling at goggling grandas,
Hairy hogs hopping happily into hurling helicopters,
Idle iguanas imagining illogical, immortal imps,
Jolly Jamaicans jabbering to jiggling Japanese jugglers,
Kings kidnapping knave kids killing kelpies with kung fu,
Latin ladies laughing loudly at labouring locksmiths,
Major mammals mangling mourning maids,
Naïve narrators negotiating with Nigerian netball players,
Obese oafs offending obstructive octopuses,
Petite pacifists painting panelled palaces,
Quirky queens questioning quoting quadruplets,
Radiant rebels racing rancid rats on ragged rapids,
Secluded scarecrows sighing seriously at seasick seals,
Tedious technicians talking tearfully to teasing teenagers,
Utmost urchins using usable uranium,
Vast vampires vanishing venom verucas on Valentine's Day,
Warbling widows washing waxwork whippets,
Xeroxes, X-rays and xylophones,
Young yachtsmen yelling at yearning youngsters,
Zealous zoologists zooming over to zany zebras.

. . . All in the new town!

**Nicola Wilson  (11)**
**Eastbank Primary School, Shettleston**

# My Grampa's Dog

My grampa's dog is mental
He's always running about
He loves to get attention
He barks when he wants out.

My grampa's dog is mental
He's about two feet tall
When he was only one month old
He was extremely small.

My grampa's dog is mental
He always makes me laugh
Once he gets in back from his walk
He has to get a bath.

My grampa's dog is mental
He drives me up the wall
When it was my birthday
He burst my brand new ball.

My grampa's dog is mental
He always runs amok
When we took him to the shop
He knocked down all the stock.

My grampa's dog is mental
He's only two years old
He like to go out for walks
Especially when it's cold.

My grampa's dog is mental
He eats everything he can see
He like to annoy everyone
Especially my cousin Leigh.

So that's the story
Of my grampa's dog
And one extra thing
He eats like a warthog.

**Alexander Coulter  (11)**
**Eastbank Primary School, Shettleston**

# The Hunt

On the hunt there are . . .

H allucinating, hairy hooligans hopping happily
U gly, unhealthy underdogs unhappily useless
N ine, notorious nasties nicknamed 'Nick'
T alkative, tattooed teens terribly tired
 I dle, ignorant intruders invading intensely
N ameless, narrow nobodies nibbling necklaces
G aunt, ghastly grandpas gloomily groaning

        . . . On the hunt.

**Hayley McIntyre (11)**
**Eastbank Primary School, Shettleston**


# My Dog

My dog
      whines when she's
          locked out
    and wags her tail
        when she's happy

My dog
      goes for a walk
         and runs about
    rounds up the
       cows then
          plays around

My dog
      is a Border collie
        still a pup
    but always will
       be called Meg
         *I love her.*

**Erin Shepherd (11)**
**Gateside Primary School, By Beith**

# Fun Fairground

The fair is fun.

I never ever lose.
I always win,
And it's so cool.

The fair is cool.
I go on all the rides,
But my brother's favourite ride is the little slide.

The fair is super.
It's super fun.
There are so many things to do,
You cannot choose.

**Wesley Smith  (9)**
**Gateside Primary School, By Beith**


# Horses

Horses can be
As brown as toast

But can also be
As white as a ghost

They like to eat oats
And when it's wet wear coats

Some like to trot
But others don't like it hot

Most like to jump
But don't like the bump

At the end of the day
They all like to play

With their friends in the field.

**Megan Reid  (11)**
**Gateside Primary School, By Beith**

# The Pleasure Beach

Steering the bumper boats
going round and round
going crazy on water.

Going on the train ride
going round and round
going over water on the little bridge.

Going on the Pepsi Max
waiting for the big drop
going up the steep hill very slow
then a big drop.

Eating lots of candyfloss
and a hot dog for my only break.

Going on the Trail Blazer, going very fast.

Going on the merry-go-round
going fast round and round,
I choose it last.

**Scott Gillan (11)**
**Gateside Primary School, By Beith**


# The Mermaid

I'm swimming, swimming in the sea,
Oh my, dearie me!
It's a mermaid, long and thin,
With a coiling, flipping fin.

She is long and thin,
*Never* pulls fishes' fins.
Has never ever kicked the wall,
Even has her own sea ball!

Her father has lots of money,
So he buys her sea honey.
She likes to eat it from a jar,
Even eats it in her car!

**Heather Gibson (8)**
**Gateside Primary School, By Beith**

# Music

Jazz, it
      puts you
            in the
                dance.

Rock, it
      puts you
            in the
                coolness.

Disco, it
      puts you
            in the
                70s.

Music, it
      puts you
            in the
                mood.

**Fabian Goldie  (8)**
**Gateside Primary School, By Beith**


# Curling On Ice

Curling stones are heavy
If you fall on the ice, it's going to be cold
So you better get training.

I used to fall but now I'm sliding.
I'm usually 1st, sometimes 2nd, never 3rd
I'm good at sweeping, I listen well.

I do what the skip tells me
I use my brush to balance when I'm sliding
And hope for the best.

**George McConnell  (10)**
**Gateside Primary School, By Beith**

# Dear, Dear Vixen

Vixen, Vixen, where did you go
Your cub is in the forest, didn't you know?
She's in danger for there are hunters about,
Vixen, oh Vixen, please get her out.

Vixen, dear Vixen, listen to the hunter's horn
But what about your cub, she's just newly born?
Oh Vixen, oh Vixen, can you hear that gun?
But Vixen, oh Vixen, they'll soon be stopping for
                                    their hot cross bun.

Vixen, dear Vixen, you are just in luck,
For there is your cub underneath that truck.
Now dear Vixen, go to your den
And listen to the church bells of Big Ben.

**Nicole Barker  (10)**
**Gateside Primary School, By Beith**


# My Puppy

My puppy
                bites me when he's angry
My puppy
                chews my stuff
My puppy
                begs when he is hungry
My puppy
                everybody says he's cute
My puppy
                loves playing
My puppy
                loves being trained
My puppy
                doesn't have fleas
*My puppy*
                *is wonderful!*

**Mollie Kerr  (9)**
**Gateside Primary School, By Beith**

# At The Beach

At the beach
　　you can make
　　　　huge sandcastles

At the beach
　　you can get
　　　　strawberry swirl ice cream

At the beach
　　you can go
　　　　snorkelling in the sea

At the beach
　　you can go
　　　　swimming in the sea

At the beach
　　you can sunbathe
　　　　on a deckchair

These are the things I love best about the beach.

**Kayleigh Brown  (9)**
**Gateside Primary School, By Beith**


# Shoes

Shoes are great
Shoes are wonderful
I love shoes and
Shoes love me
Big shoes
　　Small shoes
　　　　Giant shoes
　　　　　　Posh shoes
I loving going to the shoe shop
　　　　I love getting new shoes
　　　　　　I love all different
　　　　　　　　Types of shoes.

**Rosie McKinney  (10)**
**Gateside Primary School, By Beith**

# The Little Puppies

The little puppies
    love to eat
        and they also love to get a treat.

The little puppies
    love to jump
        over a big hump.

The little puppies
    love to spy
        with their very small eyes.

The little puppies
    love to sing
        and they like to play on the swing.

The little puppies
    love to sleep
        and they also love to leap.

**Emma Reid (9)**
**Gateside Primary School, By Beith**


# Different Plants

Plants, plants everywhere.

There're trees,
    bushes and
        weeds.

There're vegetables,
    flowers and
        herbs.

You can even have
        cacti
          or house plants.

Look after them well and they'll be

                *swell!*

**Hazel Munro (10)**
**Gateside Primary School, By Beith**

# Football

Football makes you
                        run
                                run
                                        run

Football makes it
                        fun
                                fun
                                        fun

When it is done you
        jump up and
                        run
                                run
                                        run

You like to play in the
                        sun
                                sun
                                        sun.

**Graeme Dowie (9)**
**Gateside Primary School, By Beith**


# Fairground

Spinning round on the Eclipse
when I come off I'll do the splits.

Going up and down on the Crazy Dancer
when I come off I'm like a prancer.

Once I went on the dodgems, I was hit very hard
and once I came off, I was like a bucket of lard.

I had a look at the Bomber, I thought,
*I'm not going on that because it goes up 136 feet,*
*I'll get very sick.*

**Sam Warnock (10)**
**Gateside Primary School, By Beith**

# Koala, Koala

Koala
　　Koala
　　　　with the cute little face
Koala
　　Koala
　　　　use all your pace
Koala
　　Koala
　　　　climbing that tree
Koala
　　Koala
　　　　look, there's a bee
Koala
　　Koala
　　　　with those fluffy ears
Koala
　　Koala
　　　　don't end up in tears
Koala
　　Koala
　　　　with your tiny legs
Koala
　　Koala
　　　　have you found an egg?

Koala
　　Koala
　　　　with those big brown eyes
Koala
　　Koala
　　　　I see the skies
Koala
　　Koala
　　　　sleeping fast in bed
Koala
　　Koala
　　　　sleeping with Ted.

**Aneesah Sheikh  (8)**
**Gateside Primary School, By Beith**

## The Fairground

Bomber
     Crazy Dancer
They both sound fast.

The candyfloss
     The food stalls

       They all sound sweet.

The Crazy Dancer
     The Viva Mexico
They're all different prices.

Now -
     The bingo stall, you might win something
       and you might not.

**Nicola Watson (9)**
**Gateside Primary School, By Beith**


## The Rain

Rain, rain, falls down fast
Faster than a mighty flash
I feel cold, I feel wet
I feel frozen in this set
With my gloves and with my hat
I feel like a little *cat!*

**Nathan Band (10)**
**Kennoway Primary School, Kennoway**


## The Beauty Of Water

W ater that flows in the ocean sparkling in the night.
A t night the stars gleaming on the river banks.
T ortoises that swim in the Pacific Ocean.
E verything's beautiful in the deep blue sea.
R ain that falls out of the sky, so nice.

**David Halliday (9)**
**Kennoway Primary School, Kennoway**

# Roaring Thunder

Thunder roaring in the sky

Usually in winter

It lights up the dark night sky

Everytime it is here not to play

**Megan Malcolmson (10)**
Kennoway Primary School, Kennoway


## Water In A Bottle

My
plants grow
because of the
rain. In the sky
it's used again.
It falls from clouds
into the sea.
Look at it
and what
can you see?

*Water*

**Rebecca McBeath (10)**
Kennoway Primary School, Kennoway

## An Otter

Here is an otter,
He likes to play in water,
He had a splash,
With a crash,
Here is an otter,
He likes to play in water,
He had some mash,
In a dash,
Here is an otter.

**Leona Dodds (10)**
**Kennoway Primary School, Kennoway**

## A Splash

Water,
water,
in the sky,
come and get
quickly by. Hear me
shout in a drought, 'Come
and get me out.' Water,
water in the tap, do
a big dropout
*splash!*

**Courtney Mackie (10)**
**Kennoway Primary School, Kennoway**

## Raindrops

The dirty clouds full of rain
That falls down to the ground.
It goes *drip, drip,* in the pipe.
It makes the flowers grow
And makes the fruit go ripe.

**Luke Hutchison (10)**
**Kennoway Primary School, Kennoway**

# I Love Rainy Days

Pitter-patter, hear the splatter
If I get wet it doesn't matter
It bangs on my window at night
I jump up and have a fright
I go and splash in the puddles
My mum and dad get in muddles
'You'll get all wet, get in the house'
I run in the house and splash her blouse.

      I love rainy days!

**Amy Henderson  (9)**
**Kennoway Primary School, Kennoway**


# We're Going To The Beach

We're going to the beach, beach, beach,
We need a spade each, each, each.
I'm making a letter with the sand, sand, sand.
First I get tanned, tanned, tanned.
I get buried in the sand, sand, sand.
I've hurt my hand, hand, hand.

**Kathleen Allen  (9)**
**Kennoway Primary School, Kennoway**


# At The Seaside

I went to the seaside,
there was a great tide
and I fell on my backside.
Then I went in the sea,
it was as cold as could be.
I came right out
with a great big shout.

**Marnie Lawson  (10)**
**Kennoway Primary School, Kennoway**

## Inside A Longhouse

| Orange | fire | burning |
|--------|------|---------|
| Sleeping | bed | snoring |
| Old | man | drinking |
| Mouldy | wood | smelling |
| White | flour | grinding |
| Young | man | peeking |
| Old | ladies | talking |
| Brown | buns | baking |
| Chilled | man | resting |
| Black | dog | sleeping |
| Thirsty | animals | drinking |
| Tired | slaves | snoring |
| Brown | cow | smelling |
| Young | children | playing |
| Freezing | woman | shivering. |

**Erin Smith  (9)**
**Kinellar Primary School, Blackburn**


## My Alien Limerick

I once met an alien in space
Who said he liked to trace
He tried to trace me
But fell out a tree
And now has a very squashed face.

**Joanne Findlay  (9)**
**Kinellar Primary School, Blackburn**


## My Alien Limerick

I once met an alien from Mars
Who ate a whole load of cars
He was being silly
Said his name was Billy
And he doesn't like iron bars.

**Lauren Tate  (10)**
**Kinellar Primary School, Blackburn**

# Inside A Longhouse

| | | |
|---|---|---|
| Old | man | drinking |
| Warm | lady | talking |
| Big | animals | eating |
| Smoky | wood | blazing |
| White | bread | burning |
| Big | fire | crackling |
| Three | people | freezing |
| Hot | barrels | standing |
| Little | bed | sleeping |
| Hot | smoke | flying |
| Thatch | roof | dripping. |

**Shaun MacLeod  (8)**
**Kinellar Primary School, Blackburn**


# Alien Limerick

I once met an alien from Mars
Who ate too many chocolate bars
He tripped on a hose
And broke his big nose
So he ended up washing posh cars.

**Bryce McLernon  (10)**
**Kinellar Primary School, Blackburn**


# Alien Limerick

I once saw an alien from space
His mum died in a space buggy race,
He went to the shops,
And bought Coco Pops,
And then he went back to his base.

**Alister Logie  (9)**
**Kinellar Primary School, Blackburn**

## Inside A Longhouse

| | | |
|---|---|---|
| Tiny | baby | crying |
| Huge | hailstones | falling |
| Old | man | sleeping |
| Small | pot | wiggling |
| Big | storm | thumping |
| Young | neighbours | screaming |
| Big | waves | crashing |
| Old | neighbour | shouting |
| Burnt | bread | cooling |
| Yummy | bread | disappearing |
| Soft | cattle | smelling |
| Cold | longhouse | warming |
| Small | longhouse | perfecting. |

**Rhea Barclay  (9)**
**Kinellar Primary School, Blackburn**


## My Alien Limerick

I once met an alien called Barrie
Who said he wanted to marry
He went into a bar
Met a girl in his car
And she said, 'My name is Carrie.'

**Victoria Greig  (9)**
**Kinellar Primary School, Blackburn**


## My Limerick

I once saw an alien from Spey
Who loved to dance and play
One time he got crowned
But then he drowned
And that was the end of his day.

**Holly Pirie  (9)**
**Kinellar Primary School, Blackburn**

## Inside A Longhouse

| | | |
|---|---|---|
| Hot | fire | crackling |
| Cosy | bed | snoring |
| Two | ladies | cooking |
| One | person | kneading |
| Big | bread | rising |
| Dirty | pigs | hanging |
| All | animals | smelling |
| Muddy | ground | squelching |
| Fluffy | wool | hanging |
| Cooking | utensils | sitting |
| Leather | shoes | warming |
| Young | lady | grinding. |

**Douglas Park  (9)**
**Kinellar Primary School, Blackburn**


## My Alien Limerick

I once knew an alien called Pun,
Who came from a smelly blue sun.
He ate an old cat,
And got really fat,
And now he eats all but old buns.

**Gavin McKenzie  (10)**
**Kinellar Primary School, Blackburn**


## Bob

I once knew an alien called Bob,
Who got an important job,
He quickly got fired,
Because he was tired,
And now he is a big fat blob.

**Liam Watson  (10)**
**Kinellar Primary School, Blackburn**

## Inside A Longhouse

| | | |
|---|---|---|
| Old | man | snoring |
| Young | woman | grinding |
| Ugly | pigs | snorting |
| Young | child | crying |
| Hot | pan | cooking |
| Young | man | peeking |
| Several | people | chatting |
| Old | Viking | running |
| Hot | fire | burning |
| Smelly | wood | smoking |
| Old | man | drinking |
| Ugly | woman | baking |
| Cold | floor | chilling. |

**Alexander Knapper  (9)**
**Kinellar Primary School, Blackburn**

## My Alien Limerick

There was once an alien called Murtin,
Who liked to swing on a curtain,
He flew off and crashed,
Got battered and bashed,
And where he is now is not certain.

**Martin Thomson  (10)**
**Kinellar Primary School, Blackburn**

## My Alien Limerick

I know an alien from planet Mars
Who learnt how to drive some cars
He crashed and bashed
And he didn't last
Now he is going to the stars.

**Craig Turriff  (10)**
**Kinellar Primary School, Blackburn**

# Inside A Longhouse

| Old | man | slurping |
| Smelly | animals | eating |
| Two | women | chatting |
| Smoky | fire | crackling |
| Cold | floor | itching |
| Big | bags | hanging |
| Long | benches | sitting |
| Old | man | visiting |
| Big | mess | happening |
| Huge | barrels | standing |
| Dirty | pigs | hanging |
| Big | thatch | roofing. |

**Haley Robertson (8)**
**Kinellar Primary School, Blackburn**


# Alien Limerick

There once was a guy from the sun,
He had such a lot of good fun,
But when he ate jelly,
*Kaboom!* Went his belly,
It sounded just like a shotgun!

**James Emslie (10)**
**Kinellar Primary School, Blackburn**


# My Alien Limerick

An alien once went to town
He thought a lot and bought a crown
He got a big hound
That cost just a pound
So he put on a really big frown.

**Kourtnay Wood (9)**
**Kinellar Primary School, Blackburn**

## Inside A Longhouse

| | | |
|---|---|---|
| Blazing | fire | burning |
| Cosy | bed | snoring |
| Loafy | bread | smelling |
| Fresh | water | drinking |
| Warm | smoke | steaming |
| Hot | wood | crackling |
| Old | man | shivering |
| Smelly | animals | stinking |
| Pink | pig | snorting |
| Big | longhouse | shaking. |

**Marci Harmati (9)**
Kinellar Primary School, Blackburn

## My Alien Limerick

There once was an alien from Mars,
Who said he liked monkey bars,
He took a large bite,
And got in a fight,
So now he eats chocolate cars.

**David Singer (10)**
Kinellar Primary School, Blackburn

## My Alien Limerick

There once was an alien from Mars
He liked to play in the stars
He had a big nose
And three big toes
And that's why he liked Mars bars.

**Harley Ross (10)**
Kinellar Primary School, Blackburn

# Inside A Longhouse

| Hot | fire | burning |
|-----|------|---------|
| Warm | bed | moving |
| Cosy | bread | cooking |
| Loud | voices | talking |
| Cold | people | shivering |
| Young | baby | sleeping |
| White | bread | cooking |
| Friendly | visitors | coming |
| Good | day | ending. |

**Anna Moir  (9)**
**Kinellar Primary School, Blackburn**


# Inside A Longhouse

| Little | longhouse | working |
|--------|-----------|---------|
| Older | girls | weaving |
| Small | baby | crying |
| Old | ladies | talking |
| Little | fire | smoking |
| Small | piglets | snorting |
| Hot | bread | cooling |
| Old | man | drinking |
| Big | cow | mooing. |

**Chloë Matthews  (9)**
**Kinellar Primary School, Blackburn**


# My Alien Limerick

I once saw an alien from Mars,
He drove very large, slow cars,
He had a big crash,
He got a hard bash,
And then he got hit by a bar.

**Jamie Grimbley  (10)**
**Kinellar Primary School, Blackburn**

## Inside A Longhouse

| | | |
|---|---|---|
| Murky | room | talking |
| Loving | family | living |
| Detailed | pottery | hanging |
| Fresh | bread | smelling |
| Burnt | wood | lying |
| Grubby | floor | stamping |
| Middle-age | lady | grinding |
| Old | man | dozing |
| Cold | bench | sitting |
| Dull | clothes | wearing |
| Ugly | man | staring |
| Black | wood | heating |
| Energetic | children | playing |
| Noisy | animals | standing |
| Old | man | drinking |
| Wooden | longhouse | building. |

**Ruth Ann Bryce (9)**
**Kinellar Primary School, Blackburn**


## Inside A Longhouse

| | | |
|---|---|---|
| Old | man | freezing |
| Noisy | lady | talking |
| Nosy | man | staring |
| Stretchy | dough | stringing |
| Hot | room | smoking |
| Old | lady | baking |
| Cold | animals | clattering |
| Old | bag | hanging |
| Fresh | wood | burning |
| Big | barrel | cooling |
| Old | man | staring |
| Dry | straw | crackling. |

**Tarran Eve Ross (8)**
**Kinellar Primary School, Blackburn**

# Inside A Longhouse

| | | |
|---|---|---|
| Cold | people | shivering |
| Warm | bed | sleeping |
| Cosy | fire | burning |
| Heavy | stones | churning |
| Soft | blankets | wrapping |
| Chilly | wind | blowing |
| Hot | coals | smoking |
| Burning | logs | crackling |
| Chatty | adults | talking |
| Nosy | children | listening |
| Young | baby | crying |
| Kind | girl | calming |
| Pleasant | neighbours | peeping |
| Sick | child | sobbing |
| Sore | thumb | throbbing |
| Freezing | longhouse | shaking. |

**Ailsa Macdonald  (9)**
**Kinellar Primary School, Blackburn**


# Inside A Longhouse

| | | |
|---|---|---|
| Nosy | neighbours | peeking |
| Old | ladies | talking |
| Soft | bread | baking |
| Cold | man | shaking |
| Hot | animals | smelling |
| Brown | broom | hanging |
| Fast | corn | grinding |
| Smoky | room | darkening |
| Brown | barrel | sitting |
| Old | man | drinking |
| Smoky | room | talking. |

**Hannah Thomson  (9)**
**Kinellar Primary School, Blackburn**

# Inside A Longhouse

| | | |
|---|---|---|
| White | dough | shaping |
| Cold | people | chatting |
| Brown | bread | smelling |
| Water | barrel | cooling |
| Brown | house | smoking |
| Old | man | writing |
| Hot | woman | boring |
| Dark | wood | cracking |
| Young | man | watching |
| Leather | boot | breaking |
| Mud | floor | cooling |
| Yellow | blanket | flapping |
| Pink | pig | snorting |
| Clay | pottery | standing |
| Big | boy | sneezing |
| Blind | man | touching |
| Long | house | groaning. |

**Jordan Baxter (8)**
**Kinellar Primary School, Blackburn**


# Rowan's Alien Limerick

I once saw an alien from space.
He said he was here for a race.
He just about won,
But he saw a bun,
And he has now come second place.

**Rowan Smith (10)**
**Kinellar Primary School, Blackburn**

## My Limerick

There was once an alien named Zack
Who had a big brother called Jack
He was twenty years old
And he had some gold
And his favourite colour was black.

**Rebecca Craigmile  (10)**
**Kinellar Primary School, Blackburn**

## Alien Limerick

I once saw an alien from Spain,
While he was sitting in a drain,
He started to scream,
And ate old ice cream,
Then went back to his ship again.

**Claire Mitchell  (10)**
**Kinellar Primary School, Blackburn**

## Alien Limerick

I once met an alien from Mars,
Who used to eat jam jars,
He got very fat,
And squished a cat,
And jumped at the sight of cars!

**Fergus Milne  (9)**
**Kinellar Primary School, Blackburn**

# My Alien Limerick

I once met an alien called Mack
He said he liked to smack
Because of his job
He was a green blob
And now he has learnt how to quack.

**Allison Collier  (10)**
**Kinellar Primary School, Blackburn**


# Alien Limerick

There once was an alien called Frazy,
Who ended up very lazy,
He then got a dog,
Who had a good job,
And now he is very crazy.

**Christina Robinson  (10)**
**Kinellar Primary School, Blackburn**


# Alien Limerick

I once knew an alien from Gurgle
Who said he was called Hurtle
He went to Crime Street
How he liked the beat
And now he's like moaning Myrtle.

**John Stewart  (10)**
**Kinellar Primary School, Blackburn**

## My Alien Limerick

There was once an alien called Lars,
Who came from Mars eating Mars bars,
He then ate a cat,
And got really fat,
And now he can't swing on the stars.

**Kimberley Robson  (10)**
**Kinellar Primary School, Blackburn**

## My Alien Limerick

There once came an alien from our sun,
He had a deadly big gun,
His name was Duck,
He was covered in muck,
And he loved to dance for fun!

**Euan Cruickshank  (10)**
**Kinellar Primary School, Blackburn**

## Lars

I once met an alien called Lars
I took him to an invasion on Mars
He jumped on a ship
And picked up a chip
And then he flew to the stars.

**James Williams  (9)**
**Kinellar Primary School, Blackburn**

# The Writer Of This Poem

*(Based on 'The Writer of this Poem' by Roger McGough)*

The writer of this poem
Is as tall as a pillar
As handsome as a film star
As keen as a killer

As sharp as a pencil
As cold as ice
As scary as a ghost
As fast as lice.

As happy as a chimp
As big as an oversized slug
As tricky as map reading
As fast as a bug

The writer of this poem
Is as shiny as a silk sheet
As tall as a tower
Strong enough to make you mincemeat.

**Koran Jackson  (9)**
**Kirkton of Largo Primary School, Upper Largo**

# The Writer Of This Poem

*(Based on 'The Writer of this Poem' by Roger McGough)*

The writer of this poem
Could fit in a mitten
As sweet as candy
As gentle as a kitten

As tricky as a tick
As brave as a mouse
As brainy as I can be
As happy as a house

As fast as an orbiting rocket
As cool as a disco groove
As quick as a flick
As silly as a disco move

The writer of this poem
Is as brave as a bull
Slim as a pin
But ever so cool!

**Jemma Christie (10)**
**Kirkton of Largo Primary School, Upper Largo**

# The Writer Of This Poem

*(Based on 'The Writer of this Poem' by Roger McGough)*

The writer of this poem
Is stronger than a house
As cold as a snowflake
As quiet as a mouse

As irritating as a cracking knuckle
As soft as a towel
As stupid as a woman driver
As wise as an owl

As cool as a cube of ice
As gentle as a feather
As smart as a professor
As annoying as a blether

The writer of this poem
Is always kind
He's one of twenty million billion
Or maybe I don't mind.

**Stephen Allen  (10)**
**Kirkton of Largo Primary School, Upper Largo**

# The Writer Of This Poem

*(Based on 'The Writer of this Poem' by Roger McGough)*

The writer of this poem
Is braver than a knight
As sharp as a knife
As bright as a light

As strong as a metal frame
As wise as an owl
As fast as a cheetah
As dry as a towel

As skilful as a pilot
As cool as a polar bear
As professional as a footballer
As rich as a millionaire

The writer of this poem
Is as fearsome as can be
He's as valuable as a diamond
(Or at least according to me!)

**Liam Archer (9)**
**Kirkton of Largo Primary School, Upper Largo**

# The Writer Of This Poem

*(Based on 'The Writer of this Poem' by Roger McGough)*

The writer of this poem
Is as cute as a baby
As gentle as a kiss
As polite as a lady

As crazy as the wind
As unpredictable as the sea
As beautiful as a princess
As busy as a bee

As strong as a rhinoceros
As scary as a witch
As sharp as a pencil
As irritating as an itch

The writer of this poem
Is interesting in a way
She's as changeable as the wind
(Or so I'd like to say!)

**Nyomi Band  (9)**
**Kirkton of Largo Primary School, Upper Largo**

# The Writer Of This Poem

*(Based on 'The Writer of this Poem' by Roger McGough)*

The writer of this poem
Is fuller than life
As noisy as the roar of thunder
As sharp as the blade of a knife

As quick as the flash of a camera
As smart as an eel
As brave as a soldier
As solid as steel

As strong as a ton of bricks
As tricky as a lock
As bold as a boxer
As smashing as a block

The writer of this poem
Is as happy as a bee
As sweet as honey
(That's according to me!)

**Cameron Smith  (10)**
**Kirkton of Largo Primary School, Upper Largo**

# The Writer Of This Poem

*(Based on 'The Writer of this Poem' by Roger McGough)*

The writer of this poem
Is cleverer than a cat
As fast as a fox
As brainy as a bat

As happy as a hippo
As good as a lick
As strong as a saw
As quick as a tick

As fluffy as a sheep
As tall as a tree
As sharp as a shark
As busy as a bee

The writer of this poem
Is as handsome as can be
As tricky as a fib
(But you will never see!)

**Christie McCarroll  (9)**
**Kirkton of Largo Primary School, Upper Largo**

# The Writer Of This Poem

*(Based on 'The Writer of this Poem' by Roger McGough)*

The writer of this poem
Is smarter than a bee
As slow as a slug
As brave as a flea

As bold as an athlete
As rough as the North Sea
As noisy as an elephant
As handsome as can be

As strong as a hippo
As clever as a tick
As tricky as a key
As quick as a flick

The writer of this poem
Is fascinating as can be
She's the greatest in the world
As you can see.

**Cecily Donaldson (10)**
**Kirkton of Largo Primary School, Upper Largo**

# The Writer Of This Poem

*(Based on 'The Writer of this Poem' by Roger McGough)*

The writer of this poem
Is taller than a tree
As gentle as a pillow
As thoughtful as Marie

As silly as a monkey
As funny as a clown
As happy as a dog
As nice as a crown

As cold as a piece of ice
As sharp as a knife
As slow as a snail
As far as life

The writer of this poem
Is as brave as a knight
As cool as a pool
(Or at least I think I might!)

**Morvern Gillart  (11)**
**Kirkton of Largo Primary School, Upper Largo**

# The Writer Of This Poem

*(Based on 'The Writer of this Poem' by Roger McGough)*

The writer of this poem
Is colder than ice.
As strong as a weightlifter.
As fast as lice.

As brave as a rock climber.
As sharp as a nib.
As tall as a tower.
As tricky as a fib.

As happy as helium.
As quick as a lick.
As hot as Spain.
As clever as a trick.

The writer of this poem
Is as good as gone.
As brainy as a science professor.
(But stay off his lawn!)

**Innis MacLeod  (10)**
**Kirkton of Largo Primary School, Upper Largo**

# The Writer Of This Poem

*(Based on 'The Writer of this Poem' by Roger McGough)*

The writer of this poem
Is smaller than a door
As cold as ice
As sharp as a lawnmower

As fast as a bird
As tricky as a rat
As sweet as a pea
As long as a mat

As tangly as a lion's mane
As brave as a bat
As annoying as an itch
As keen as a cat

The writer of this poem
Is worth a pound
As glamorous as a girl
But never makes a sound.

**Abbie Clunie (10)**
**Kirkton of Largo Primary School, Upper Largo**

# The Writer Of This Poem

*(Based on 'The Writer of this Poem' by Roger McGough)*

The writer of this poem
Is harder than a brick
As happy as a hippo
As good as a lick

As nice as an ice cream
As sweet as a pea
As light as rain
As busy as a bee

As brown as a baboon
As funny as a fish
As orange as Irn-Bru
As great as a wish

The writer of this poem
Is as tall as a tree
As long as a snake
(According to me!)

**Indica McCabe  (9)**
**Kirkton of Largo Primary School, Upper Largo**

# The Writer Of This Poem

*(Based on 'The Writer of this Poem' by Roger McGough)*

The writer of this poem
Is taller than a tower
As bouncy as a ball
As pretty as a flower.

As sour as a lemon
As sweet as a pea
As funny as a clown
As busy as a bee.

As clumsy as a kangaroo
As small as a bug
As bright as the sunshine
As slimy as a slug.

The writer of this poem
Is as brainy as can be
She's the greatest ever.
(Well, according to me!)

**Holly Rennie (8)**
**Kirkton of Largo Primary School, Upper Largo**

## My Special Possession Kennings

Best-cuddler
eye-catcher
great-player
night-sleeper

good-nuzzler
best-wisher
hay-muncher
day-grazer

hoof-trotter
shed-lover
big-feet
great-traveller
love-Jenners
friend-maker.

**Tessa Kilpatrick (7)**
**Law Primary School, North Berwick**


## My Dog Alfie

A food-muncher
A good-bouncer
A cute-killer
A red-fur ball
A roller-poller
A tough-terroriser
A cuddly-kisser
A rabbit-chaser
A ball-catcher
A scratcher-stroller
A big-biter
A beanbag-lover.

**Eve Milne (8)**
**Law Primary School, North Berwick**

# My Special Possession Is My . . . Kennings

Tease-people
lock them-up
play-cowboys
frighten-them
hit-people
heavy-metal
not-friendly
from-Jedburgh
not-fake
wrist-hurter
not-snappable
police-weapon
locker-upper
reflection-show-er
show-offer.

**Lewis Grant  (8)**
**Law Primary School, North Berwick**


# My Carrot-Muncher Kennings

Cuddle-liker
carrot-muncher
energetic-runner
water-sucker
apple-chomper
hutch-lover
warm-cuddler
sleep-lover
food-scoffer
high-jumper
white-fur ball
active-player.

**Katie Bennett  (8)**
**Law Primary School, North Berwick**

# My Special Possession Kennings

Playing-master
walk-handler
toilet-rusher
leg-brusher
bark-maker
cleaning-machine
tail-biter
ball-catcher
shadow-chaser
hole-digger
jumping-mad
night-whiner
best-friend
food-hater
book-destroyer
Speedy-Gonzales.

**Liam Mackle  (8)**
**Law Primary School, North Berwick**


# My Special Possession

Long-tailed
soft as silk
mouse-killer
flea-house
purr-maker
daytime-doser
relaxer-inspirer
long-whiskered
thick-furred
eating-machine
fly-catcher
night-time-exerciser.

**Victoria Duncan-Timpson  (8)**
**Law Primary School, North Berwick**

# My Special Possession

Night prowler and a great hunter
a great hunter
a cream licker
a great player
a food taker
a sneaky thing
a soft cuddler
a sharp biter
a fast runner
a mouse chaser
a night sleeper
a dog chaser
a great brush
good hugger
a flea's home.

**Lily Armstrong  (7)**
**Law Primary School, North Berwick**


# My Special Possession Kennings

Soft-cuddler
game-maker
fun-player
colourful-show-offer
furry-friend
explore-traveller
activity-finder
eye-catching
time-passer
birthday-toys
I take it everywhere I go.

**Fenella Walker  (7)**
**Law Primary School, North Berwick**

# My Special Possession Is My Pig Family

Cuddle-makers
friendly-friends
softie-friends
cute-cuddlers
sweet-huggers
big-huggers
beautiful-admirers.

**Charlotte Forbes**
**Law Primary School, North Berwick**

# My Special Possession Kennings

Milk-licker
daytime-sleeper
speedy-legs
house-animal
my-friend
purr-maker
good-reflexes
white-black
guinea pig-friend.

**Findlay Graham (8)**
**Law Primary School, North Berwick**

# My Special Possession Kennings

Animal-killer
lethal-weapon
time-waster
nice-design
special-present
from-Australia.

**Michael Bell (8)**
**Law Primary School, North Berwick**

# My Special Person Kennings

Time-passer
big-bouncer
good-shouter
good-runner
good-jumper
funny-animal
good-roller
funny-sleeper.

**Ryan Thomson  (8)**
**Law Primary School, North Berwick**


# My Special Possession Is . . .

A Man City supporter
a big squasher
a licker machine
a fluffy little thing
she can't see properly
but she's still cuddly and snuggly
she kisses a lot
but she's a mouse killer.

**Michael Dean  (8)**
**Law Primary School, North Berwick**


# Fur Ball Kennings

Grass and cabbage muncher
black fur ball
best friend
cuddler
fast runner
Olympic jumper
a big softie
dream hypnotiser.

**Martha Kemp  (8)**
**Law Primary School, North Berwick**

# The Mystery Animal Kennings

Feed-gulper
sticky bud-finder
water-lapper
mini-howler
football-puncturer
leg-brusher
rabbit-hunter
licker-facer
black-swoosh.

**Kathryn Wilson (8)**
**Law Primary School, North Berwick**


# My Special Possession

Soft-cuddler
bed-liver
football-dreamer
eight-fiddler
big-rustler
mini-tiger
great-friend
travelling-companion.

**John Gardner (8)**
**Law Primary School, North Berwick**


# My Special Possession

I play with it.
I display on my shelf.
She's beautiful with her long, flowing dress.
A Greek goddess.
She's got long gold hair.
I treasure her.

**Sophie Egert (7)**
**Law Primary School, North Berwick**

## My Special Possession

It's my favourite hobby,
I can get a lot of fresh air,
I've won three competitions,
I'd like to get a hole in one,
I get lots of lessons,
A lot of exercise playing,
Sometimes I get bad holes,
I like playing with my friends.

**Finlay Goodlad (7)**
**Law Primary School, North Berwick**


## My Special Possession

Active looker
fun to play with
she's from Russia
she's very precious
she has a long dress
she has a small hat on her head.

**Ruth Elias**
**Law Primary School, North Berwick**


## My Dogs

My dogs, my dogs,
They love to play,
They are lovely and cuddly,
But they love to run away!

Connie, Heidi and Flora too,
I let them out,
When they need the loo!

**Andrew James Grant-Suttie (8)**
**Law Primary School, North Berwick**

# My Special Possessions Kennings

Time-passer
mini-tail
active-player
fast-eater
great-watcher
beautiful-eyes
great-colour
black-white
mouse-brother
show-offer
sleep-day
love-himself
active-night
food-gulper
couch-chewer.

**Heather Oberlander  (8)**
**Law Primary School, North Berwick**


# My Special Possession Kennings

Show-offer
Silver-show-offer
Proud-displayer
It is shiny and silvery
It is big
I won it
Big-silvery
Huge-shiny
Displayful
Good-improved.

**Beth Lauder  (8)**
**Law Primary School, North Berwick**

# Glower Ball Of Light

Show-offer
Keep-safer
25-edger
25-facer
40-cornerer
Rainbow-reflectioner
Foot-dropper
Juggle-shaper
Special-possession
Encourage-point
Make me stronger
Dream-maker
Nightmare-stopper
Glower ball of light
What is it?
It is a crystal.

**Cameron Robertson  (8)**
**Law Primary School, North Berwick**


# My Special Possessions Kennings

Moth-catcher
tail-licker
inspiring-creature
warm-coated
rescued-orphan
tail-flicker
foot-licker
time-ticker
moth-kicker
long-stretcher
love-fetcher
kiss-catcher.

**Eoin Patrick  (8)**
**Law Primary School, North Berwick**

# My Special Possession Kennings

Little stealer
fast eater
belly scratcher
nice colour
cool style
fast runner
high jumper
ball catcher
little builder.

**Joshua Stewart (8)**
**Law Primary School, North Berwick**


# Spring

S pring is the best season
P ink blossom on the trees
R acing to come out
I n the leaves are ants
N ine leaves are out
G etting there all the time.

**Sophie Ferguson (8)**
**Law Primary School, North Berwick**


# My Boat

A sail colourful and bright,
A flipper wet and soggy,
A bird so elegant in flight,
A fish thrown to a pile,
A stool painted green,
A rod flung up to the air
Back down to sea!
All on my fishing boat.

**Esther Borsi (7)**
**Law Primary School, North Berwick**

# School Time

Come out the door
Run to your friend's
Eat your snack
Play your games
Never rest till the bell goes
Do your work home time's soon
There's the bell
Out the door, run to your mum
Get into the car and drive away
Tomorrow you'll be back.

**Abigail Pooley (7)**
**Law Primary School, North Berwick**

# The Earthworm

Earthworms, earthworms twirl and whirl
Running away from the crows that flow
People think that they are mad
They are insane and have no laugh
Big and never look the same
Especially when they curl away
So tight that you never see them again.

**Matthew Watt (8)**
**Law Primary School, North Berwick**

# Chocolate

Chocolate chocolate in the shop.
Chocolate we need some.
Chocolate we like the taste.
Chocolate yum-yum.
Chocolate chocolate just for you.
Come on have a chew.

**Adam Naylor (8)**
**Law Primary School, North Berwick**

# The Hamster And The Black Cat

The big, furry, black cat,
Stares down on the hamster's back,
Hamster comes up on top of the cage,
Walking steadily on to the stage.
Nip! Hamster bites his paw,
Such a big humongous jaw,
Black cat jumps with a fright,
That was quite a big bad bite!

**Isla Menneer (8)**
**Law Primary School, North Berwick**

# Caterpillars

Caterpillars caterpillars in your hair
Caterpillars caterpillars everywhere
Caterpillars caterpillars in your underwear
Colourful caterpillars on the trees
Trying to catch lots of fleas
Caterpillars caterpillars can be a pest
So stop trying to catch them, give it a rest.

**Thomas Brogden (7)**
**Law Primary School, North Berwick**

# Playground Poetry

B ig and yellow bananas
A lways peel off the skin!
N ever smash a banana!
A new banana is very tasty
N ever eat the skin!
A big banana will do for me!

**Hamish Barbour (8)**
**Law Primary School, North Berwick**

# Cricket

Cricket ball whizzing through the air
bowled by a mysterious black bear.

Bails crashing to the ground bowled
by a ghastly brown greyhound.

Billy Bowden raising his crooked finger
saying, 'Out!' loudly. Never linger.

**Michael Hagan  (8)**
**Law Primary School, North Berwick**


# Ants

A nts here ants there, ants in your skin
N aughty and silly ants creeping all over
T all and small but never angry
S lowly and even slower while the day goes out.

**Riccardo Cucchi  (8)**
**Law Primary School, North Berwick**


# Autumn - Haiku

Conkers on the ground
The conkers are really brown
They are shiny round.

**Jade Munro  (8)**
**Leslie Primary School, Leslie**


# Autumn - Haiku

Branches smell of peas
Conkers shiny chestnut brown
Leaves brown and yellow.

**Carla Blakey  (9)**
**Leslie Primary School, Leslie**

# Autumn - Haiku

A tall holly tree,
Dropping berries on the ground,
With big jaggy leaves.

**Rachel Gould  (9)**
**Leslie Primary School, Leslie**

# Autumn - Haiku

Hedgehogs hibernate
To a house, spiders migrate
Squirrels collect nuts.

**Kirsty Drysdale  (9)**
**Leslie Primary School, Leslie**

# Autumn - Haiku

With leaves orange-red
A big tall colourful tree
Dropping its conkers.

**Chloe McCaffery  (9)**
**Leslie Primary School, Leslie**

# Autumn - Haiku

A tall conker tree.
On a tree, different colours.
The berries are red.

**Lilybeth Paterson  (8)**
**Leslie Primary School, Leslie**

## Autumn - Haiku

Mushrooms brown and cream
Soft and rounded on the ground
Edible mushrooms.

**Evie Cumming  (9)**
**Leslie Primary School, Leslie**


## Autumn - Haiku

The tall conker tree.
Conkers grow in shells on trees.
They are round and brown.

**Keiren Martin  (9)**
**Leslie Primary School, Leslie**


## Autumn - Haiku

The tall sycamore.
It's big and too high to climb
And it smells rotten.

**Akram Basha  (9)**
**Leslie Primary School, Leslie**


## Autumn - Haiku

Crunchy crunch go leaves
lying on the ground crumpled
yellow, red and brown.

**Amy Gordon  (9)**
**Leslie Primary School, Leslie**

# Autumn

When the leaves sway on the trees,
You know there's going to be a breeze.
Squirrels collecting,
Farmers harvesting,
Leaves are falling down.

Go inside to get some warmth,
Mum goes off to make some broth.
On an autumn day,
No one out to play,
Instead they're inside to stay.

**Lydia Stephen (9)**
**Maud School, Maud**


# Autumn

A ll the leaves are falling from the trees
U nder the trees are some leaves
T urning orange, red, yellow, gold and brown
U p above the trees are getting bare
M aking big piles of leaves
N early winter now.

**James Scott (7)**
**Maud School, Maud**


# Harvest

H ow busy are the farmers?
A ll gathering in the barley
R ipe fruit
V ery juicy apples
E very farmer is working hard
S till to finish
T hen it's time for dinner.

**Jody McGregor (7)**
**Maud School, Maud**

# Autumn

Swirling, twirling
Leaves falling
Red and golden
Wondering, dancing, crunching

Leaves to throw
Leaves to kick
All slimy when wet
Crisp when dry.

Autumn.

**Kelsey Burnett (11)**
Maud School, Maud

# Harvest

H appy joys, it's autumn time again
A ll the farmers are storing up the corn
R eady to eat all the juicy apples
V ery cloudy, windy and rainy, very bad weather
E verything looks golden and ripe
S toring all the autumn food
T ime for the squirrels to hibernate.

**Aimee Mowat (7)**
Maud School, Maud

# Autumn

Autumn is here
Summer is gone
It's starting to get cold
Now let's get warm

Leaves are falling from the trees
Orange, gold and brown too
Swirling, twirling from the trees
To the ground.

**Kelly Paterson (11)**
Maud School, Maud

# Autumn

Twirling, swirling, fluttering,
Leaves in the air,
It's autumn again,
So put your hands in the air.

Twirling, swirling, fluttering,
It's cold again,
The birds are chirping,
On the trees that are bare.

The machines are working overdrive,
Gathering the harvest before it's too late,
The dormice are scuttling across the field,
Twirling, swirling, fluttering.

**Cameron Buchan (9)**
**Maud School, Maud**


# Autumn

A ll the animals hibernate
U nder the red and yellow leaves
T ime to go to sleep for wintertime
U p above the squirrels store nuts
M aking food for the wintertime
N ow the trees are bare.

**Stephanie-Louise Wilson (7)**
**Maud School, Maud**


# Autumn

A ll the leaves are falling from the trees
U nder the trees there are lots of leaves
T he leaves are turning orange, red, yellow and gold
U ntil they swirl and fall to the ground
M any animals are hibernating
N ow the trees are bare.

**Ela McDougall (7)**
**Maud School, Maud**

# Autumn

Trees are bare
Leaves are fluttering in the air
Golden leaves begin to crunch
So people pile them up in a bunch
Animals store up on their food
Away to sleep but not for good
Farmers combining the straw and grain
Farmers baling again and again
The grain gets dried and stored
Children inside getting bored.

**Iain Birnie  (10)**
**Maud School, Maud**


# It's Autumn Again

It's autumn again
And leaves are falling off the trees
Leaves are swirling, twirling
In the breeze
The nights are dark and cold
But through the day
I will go outside and watch
The beautiful leaves
Twirl and swirl in the air.

**Faye Cruickshank  (9)**
**Maud School, Maud**


# Autumn

In autumn leaves twirl
and swirl in the breezy wind,
like fluttering helicopters

Crispy leaves are falling off trees
like dancing bears
dancing in the air.

**Megan Will  (9)**
**Maud School, Maud**

# Autumn Poem

The autumn wind.
The farmers harvest the crops.
The golden leaves that fall.
The little children jump in leaves in delight.
The golden sunshine lights up the sky.
The squirrels are gathering food.
Field mice look for food in he fields.
Nights get darker.
Air gets colder.

**Alexander Paterson  (9)**
Maud School, Maud


# Autumn

It is chillier than summer
Swirling, twirling, fluttering leaves
Animals are hibernating
The nights are even longer
I want to sleep longer

All the birds are flying
To a warm part of the world
Just until the winter's over.

**Jasmine Matthews  (10)**
Maud School, Maud


# Autumn

Swirling, fluttering leaves
Stacked up bales
Newly cut fields
Squirrels gathering nuts
Chill in the air
Twigs flying down
The rev of tractors
All in autumn.

**Matthew Paterson  (11)**
Maud School, Maud

# My Harvest Poem

Soft golden leaves blow in the wind
piling and falling on each other
in the darkness
badgers and hedgehogs hibernating

Birds singing in the breeze
all day long
drifting and gliding through the air
badgers and hedgehogs hibernating

Children jumping and collecting leaves
conkers are falling from the trees
clattering on the ground
badgers and hedgehogs hibernating

Nights are longer
the winds are stronger
there's a chill in the air
badgers and hedgehogs hibernating.

**James Greig  (10)**
**Maud School, Maud**


# Autumn

A cold autumn
golden leaves resting on the ground
bales round and square stacked in the shed
tractors, combines and lorries cutting in the fields
going backwards and forwards

Shepherds taking in their flock
floats running from field to farm

The smell of fresh grain invades the air
dryers working here and there
a slight chill nips the air.

**James Hay  (10)**
**Maud School, Maud**

# Autumn

Autumn is here, the wind is about,
Everyone in, nobody out,
As the leaves drift off the trees,
Swirling down right to the ground,
The children finally come out to play
Because they're used to the autumn day,
Stack up the leaves into a pile,
Have a jump, show us some style,
Autumn is here and the wind is about,
Everyone in, nobody out.

**Ryan Cameron  (11)**
**Maud School, Maud**


# Autumn

A ll the leaves fall off the trees
U p above the twigs are bare
T urning orange, red, yellow and gold
U nder the trees are loads of leaves
M any haystacks in the field
N early, it will be winter.

**Sam Graham  (7)**
**Maud School, Maud**


# The Tiger!

This is Tiger, big and strong,
He's orange and black,
With stripes upon his back,
While his prey are in a riot,
He'll creep up and be so quiet,
When suddenly *roar!* - He pounces out,
Now there'll be no prey about!
So now he will just have to sleep;
And he will sleep without a peep!

**Rachael Robertson  (11)**
**Mile End Primary School, Aberdeen**

# India!

It's sizzling
It's boiling hot
Like spicy curry in a copper pot
With yummy spices . . .
Yum! Yum! Yum!
After 10 minutes
It's in my tum.

The tiger roars
Its black eyes gleaming
The snake goes hiss
Its venom steaming
The monkey swings
In the tall, green trees
Going ooh, ooh, ahh!
In the cool, swift breeze.

Bollywood stars go,
La la la!
Movie directors go
Cut cut cut!
The audience go
Ha ha ha!
The movie critics go
Yuck!

Give me an I
    an N
     a D
      I
      A
What does that spell?
        *India.*

**Sarah Rahman  (10)**
**Mile End Primary School, Aberdeen**

# Haikus Of Indian Food

*Curry*

Curry, curry, yum,
Tikka masala is fine,
Rice and chicken too!

*Rice is very nice*

Rice is very nice,
So is naan bread with hot sauce
Spicy eggs are nice!

*Desserts*

Desserts are good there,
The iced dessert looks lovely,
Great food, India!

**Scott Mackie  (11)**
**Mile End Primary School, Aberdeen**


# Rivers In India

The River Ganges flows
All over India and Bangladesh
Past Calcutta and into the sea
That is the River Ganges!

The River Indus
Starts in India and
Flows through Pakistan
And into the Arabian sea!

Rivers in India
Are majestic
People washing beside them
Saying, 'Oh Shiva please help me!'

**Finlay Johnston  (11)**
**Mile End Primary School, Aberdeen**

# This Is India

T his is India
H imalayas are covered in snow most of the year
I n India people like curry
S ome people go to the cinema

I n villages bullock cart races are played
S ome people are poor and have to live in shanty towns

I n fields rice is collected
N ow crops are dying
D ubba wallahs deliver tiffin boxes
I n monsoon season the rain is warm
A nd that is my poem about India.

**Kenneth Will  (10)**
**Mile End Primary School, Aberdeen**


# Indian Lifestyle

India, India, 'O' sweet India
Like us but we're windier
I might send you a letter
About who's wetter
I'll see you soon
Hopefully not in the monsoon
Your food is good
I hope I'm not rude
I like curry
But it costs lots of money
I hear rupee is your currency
I think it looks fancy
An autorickshaw
I think that's what I saw
It was driving to school
Boy it looked cool!

**Nicholas Logan  (11)**
**Mile End Primary School, Aberdeen**

# I'm Happy Anyway

I ain't got marbles
And I ain't got toys,
My village is quiet
And there ain't any noise.

It's a pretty normal day,
But I'm still happy anyway.

The sun is beating down on my head,
All our crops and fields are dead.

It's a pretty normal day,
But I'm still happy anyway.

Clip-clop go the bullock-carts,
Fast as lightning or poison darts.

It's a pretty normal day,
But I'm still happy anyway.

Monsoon rain is falling down,
Landing on my head,
Like a silver crown.

It's a pretty normal day,
But I'll enjoy it anyway.

**Ellen Shand (10)**
**Mile End Primary School, Aberdeen**

# Village Life In India

Bullet carts are stomping
Autorickshaws are driving
People are working

*Village life in India*

Everyone fetching water
Pot makers for dishes
Weavers for clothes

*Village life in India*

People picking rice
Fishing rods are swinging
Streams are flowing

*Village life in India*

People growing crops
Puppet shows entertain
Very few shops

*Village life in India.*

**Matthew John Greer (11)**
**Mile End Primary School, Aberdeen**

# India's Food

Curry, curry, it rhymes with Murray
He hasn't even tried it yet
He lies and lies
But still he cries
The unbelievable taste
That tastes unbelievably great

But don't forget the scrambled egg
The mouth-watering taste
That is so great
It can be smelt from a mile away
It sends Murray running
To taste its spice
The second he puts it
In his mouth
He thinks he's floating
On a cloud.

**Sammy Anindo  (11)**
**Mile End Primary School, Aberdeen**

# Tiger - Haikus

*Another tiger*

Another tiger,
Killed by a heartless hunter.
Just for the money.

*Black and orange*

Striped black and orange
Creeping through the dense jungle,
This is the tiger.

*Its beautiful fur*

Its beautiful fur,
Accompanied by a purr.
Tigers are so great.

**David Hewitt  (11)**
**Mile End Primary School, Aberdeen**

# I Believe

I am a Hindu,
I have a shrine,
I say a prayer, just one line.

I believe in Shiva,
Because he is a diva,
Shiva is the preserver god,
He treads on the dwarf of ignorance.

I believe in Hanuman,
Because he is the god of intelligence,
He helped the prince Rama,
Or do I believe in Brahma?

I believe in Vishnu,
Because he protects the Earth,
He has blue skin,
I think he wins.

**Keira Napier  (11)**
**Mile End Primary School, Aberdeen**


# The Little Man In India

The little man in India
Lived on a little farm
The little farm in India
Had a little patch of rice
The little patch of rice
Had a little person picking
The little person picking
Saw a little little horse
The little little horse
Had a little little foal
The little little foal
Had a little little teddy
The little little teddy
Was called little Bill.

**Connor Anderson  (11)**
**Mile End Primary School, Aberdeen**

# The Indian Rainforest

Baboons eat spiders
They taste like cider.
Monsoons pour down
And drench the ground.
Venom makes denim
Dissolve like paper.
Snakes awake taking
Pies in the making.
Ant running riot
Being very quiet.
Poison dart frogs
Hog the bogging log.
The local animals
Don't have keys
All they have is really big trees.
Local people eat lots of fish
But they wish it was on a big dish.

All these things are the Indian rainforest.
Chop it down and they'll all die.

**Campbell Simpson  (10)**
**Mile End Primary School, Aberdeen**

# Indian Food

Rice is nice
Covered with spice
Curry is hot
When cooked in a pot
Fruit is fine
Covered in lime
This is India's ace food.

Naan bread is nice
Dipped into curry spice
Banana leaves blooming
Food on it gleaming
This is India's ace food.

Indian nights
Must be so nice
If they have all this Indian spice
Would you like to eat all this spice?
This is India's ace food.

**Cameron Howe  (10)**
**Mile End Primary School, Aberdeen**

# My World And Yours

I n India I wake up at 6am at dawn, tired from the night before
N ext me and Mum go down to the well with buckets made of wood
heavy as a tree
D own to market I go for a basket full of spice, a tiny town buzzing
with life and energy
I 'm happy because my gran has come to tell me tales of long ago
as I eat chapatis full of curry
A t the end of the day the sky is pink, a glowing sun about to sink,
as I go into dreamy sleep at 8pm

A busy city full of life as I wake, the traffic stirs
B y 9am I'm in my school and I think it is very cool
E verything is good and so is the food, sandwiches, pasta,
whatever you like
R eady for the afternoon and drama's coming next, mimicking,
miming or performing?
D own to town I go to Asda or Tesco, an endless food store with
anything you want
E lephant sized houses neatly made with stone, the flat, the red, the
speckled or grey.
E verybody's different, the blonde and the brown, the light and the
dark, the freckled and the not!

N ever, ever boring, rarely nothing to do, this is Aberdeen calling
to you!

**Clare Armstrong  (10)**
**Mile End Primary School, Aberdeen**

# Monsoon Seasons

M onsoon seasons are very wet
O ver the first half of the monsoon, rain grows heavier
N othing escapes the heavy rain
S plish! Splash! go the puddles
O n some fields, crops are growing healthily
O thers are dying and the farmers are not happy
N one of the days don't have rain.

S ome people are in such a rush, they forget an umbrella
E veryone except children have umbrellas
A ll people get soaked
S oaking leaves drip on people's heads
O n the monsoon season, the Thar Desert hardly gets any rain
N early all the children like the monsoon
S ome children don't.

**Joseph Lawson (10)**
**Mile End Primary School, Aberdeen**

# Indian Animals

Monkeys swinging through the trees
Elephants trumpeting too
The tiger stalking its prey
These are India's animals.

The spiders are spinning a shiny web
The snakes are slithering through the grass
Gorillas grasping lots of bananas
These are India's animals.

In the desert the scorpion hides
Waiting for a lizard to pass
These are India's animals.

In the jungle the leopard jumps from tree to tree
Chasing the wild boar
These are India's animals.

**Murray Gauld (11)**
**Mile End Primary School, Aberdeen**

# What Shall We See?

'What shall we see?
What shall we see?

Let's look for tigers,
Hiding in the grass,
Look at the rice fields,
People working fast.

What shall we see?
What shall we see?

Brilliant Bollywood dancers
Dancing in the street.
What a big traffic jam,
Where all cars meet.

What shall we see?
What shall we see?

Look at the puppets
Telling their tales,
Look those speeding bull carts,
Careful cling tight to the rails.

What shall we see?
What shall we see?

Oh no, here comes the rain
Come on, quick or we'll miss the train!'

**Melissa Smart  (11)**
**Mile End Primary School, Aberdeen**

# The Season Of Rain

This afternoon
was the start of the monsoon.
It bucketed down,
but I didn't put on a frown.
I was a happy
little chappy.

I had a shower
in the rain.
Fun is very easy
to obtain.
I splashed in puddles
most of the day.
I enjoyed today
because all I did was play.

Still it rains
three and a half months later.
The depths of puddles
still grows greater.
Two weeks afterwards
a rainbow appears.
Now, the sky is clear.
There is no more rain.

**Gavin Thomas (10)**
**Mile End Primary School, Aberdeen**

# The Bengal Tiger

Lily was striding through the jungle,
When something caught her eye.
She spun to her right
And gazed at a tiger ambling by.

His eyes were fixed before him,
His ruthless, black eyes glistening under the sun.
His vicious claws were silently moving
And suddenly he broke into a swift, smooth run.

Lily tailed the tiger.
She ran past pestilential chimpanzees,
Cute little monkeys,
And beautiful, deciduous trees.

Then she stumbled over a great big log.
The tiger stopped in his tracks and released a furious roar.
He slowly turned and looked at her with a wicked glint in his eyes.
Then, Lily ran and ran and ran until she could run no more.

**Mugdha Nagrath  (11)**
**Mile End Primary School, Aberdeen**

# A Rainforest Rhyme

I was driving along in my Jaguar
When I heard a noise going, *'Rar rar rar.*
*What's up! Yo bro!'*

It was a jaguar and its name was Kevin G.
It was prowling around and it looked at me.
Cool dude! Wicked!

I hit the accelerator, come on let's go
And it still said, 'What's up! Yo bro!
Yo yo! What's up!'

I put my foot down and I drove away off,
I had so much fuel he went cough cough cough!
See ya! *Broom!*

**Jennifer Ramsay  (9)**
**Rattray Primary School, Rattray**

# Rainforest

*Morning!*

The sun rose like a boiling snooker ball
    Floating over the Amazon
        Rain dripped like blood
            Splashing on the bird-eating tarantulas
              Steam rises like a ghostly mist
                Awakening the sleeping
                  Monkey roar
                *Morning!*

*Nightfall!*

The moon rises like a five-pence coin
    Drifting across hummingbirds that sit on the trees
        Darkness creeps like black widow spiders
            Covering the forest floor
              Nocturnal creatures crawl like lizards.

**Jamie Mckinlay (10)**
**Rattray Primary School, Rattray**


# Rainforest Poem

*Morning*

The sun rose like a
burning circle of bright red
floating over the golden land
drifting through the burning hot, golden beach
It is as hot as the burning hot sun

*Nightfall*

The moon shines as a white
golf ball drifting through darkness
creeps like a black Goth moving everywhere
I see nocturnal creatures crawl like a
dark black, hairy tarantula
              *Nightfall.*

**Jonathan Kermath (10)**
**Rattray Primary School, Rattray**

# Rainforest

*Morning!*

The sun rose like golden grains of sand,
Floating like a swooping toucan
Rain dripped like an oil leak
Splashing on the evergreen leaves
Steam rises like water on a cooker
Disguising as a lazy leopard
Awakening the sleeping sloth
*Raah! Squawk!*

*Nightfall!*

The moon rises like a wine top
Drifting across the prey of a black panther
Darkness creeps like a flying bat
Covering the snoring sloth
Nocturnal creatures crawl like a creeping spider
Waiting for its prey
*Grr! Hoot hoot!*

**Christie Comrie (9)**
**Rattray Primary School, Rattray**

# Rainforest

*Morning!*

The sun rose like a fiery-red snooker ball,
Floating over all the sleeping animals,
The rain dripped like a giant's tears,
Slashing on the monkeys, keeping them cool.
Steam rises like a boiling kettle,
Disguising all the hunting jaguars,
Awakening all the moaning monkeys.
*Roar! Squawk! Roar!*
            *Morning!*

*Nightfall!*

The moon rose like a five-pence coin,
Drifting across the evergreen trees,
Darkness creeps like a black panther,
Covering the forest floor so it's pitch-black.
Nocturnal creatures crawl slowly
Waiting for prey to go past.

**Melissa Harper  (9)**
**Rattray Primary School, Rattray**

# Rainforest

*Morning!*

The sun rose like a blazing fireball,
Floating over the animal kingdom.
Rain dripped like hailstones,
Splashing on the overflowing Amazon.
Steam rises like the sun rising,
Disguising the lazy-legged animals.
Awakening the sleeping, squawking birds.
*Roar! Squeak! Squeal!*

*Nightfall!*

The moon rises like a burnt football,
Drifting across the Amazon River.
Darkness creeps like a black widow,
Covering the panther's black fur.
Nocturnal creatures crawl like marching ants,
Waiting to ambush its prey.
*Hoot! Scream! Growl!*

**Wayne Osborne  (11)**
**Rattray Primary School, Rattray**

# Rainforest

Morning
The sun rises like a yellow football of fire
Floating across the bright blue sky
Rain dripped like a lion's teardrops
Splashing into the monkey's eye
Steam rises like a grey foggy cloud
Disguising the terrifying camouflaged tigers
Awakening the sleepy lazy monkeys
*Hiss! Quack! Squack!*
Morning.

Nightfall.
The moon rises like a shiny silver coin
Drifting across the shadows of trees
Darkness creeps like a white silver shadow
Covering the forest floor
Nocturnal creatures crawl like sneaky spiders
Waiting to catch their prey with a snap
*Hoot! Scream! Growl!*
Nightfall.

**Connor Buchanan  (10)**
**Rattray Primary School, Rattray**

# Rainforest

*Morning!*

The sun rose like a burning beach ball
Floating over the sleeping rainforest
Rain dripped like a lion's tears.
Splashing on the tiger's woolly coat
Steam rises like a bed of fog.
Disguising the blue and green lizard
Awakening the sleeping silky sloths
*Roar! Squeak! Screech!*
                    *Morning!*

*Nightfall!*

The moon rises like a silver alloyed rim
Drifting across the River Amazon.
Darkness creeps like a dark black shadow
Covering the eagles' sleeping nests.
Nocturnal creatures crawl like an ant army
Waiting for unsuspecting, tasty prey.
*Hoot! Scream! Growl!*
                    *Nightfall!*

**Robert Willemars  (10)**
**Rattray Primary School, Rattray**

# Rainforest

*Morning!*

The sun rose like a ball of fire
Floating over the Amazon
Rain drips like snowdrops
Splashing on a sleeping lion
Steam rises like candyfloss over the Amazon
Disguising the tree frogs in the trees
Awakening the lion.
              *Morning!*

*Nightfall!*

The moon rises like a wheel
Darkness creeps like a black cat
Covering the forest floor
Nocturnal creatures crowd like a snake
Waiting for its food.
              *Nightfall!*

**Jack Bruce  (10)**
**Rattray Primary School, Rattray**

# Rainforest

*Morning!*

The sun rose like a blazing beach ball,
Floating over the evergreen trees.
Rain dripped like God's tears,
Splashing on the animals and plants.
Steam rises like candyfloss in the canopy,
Disguising the sinking sand.
Awaken the annoyed armadillo!
*Roar! Grr! Cheep!*
                    *Morning!*

*Nightfall!*

The moon moves like a silver river,
Drifting across the fruit bat.
Darkness creeps like a tiger,
'Squeak! Squeak!' says the rat.
Creeping along the ground,
Covering the armadillo are leaves.
Under the leaves the armadillo sleeps,
The awaiting panther is waiting for its meal.
*Eek! Roar! Squeak!*
                    *Nightfall!*

**Cara Henderson  (9)**
**Rattray Primary School, Rattray**

# Rainforest Day

*Morning!*

The sun rose like a glowing golden orb,
Drifting over a sea of green,
Rain dripped like a river of tears,
Splashing like a bottle of suncream,
Steam rises like warmed liquid nitrogen,
Disguising the land in a silvery cloak,
Awakening the sleeping land!
*Roar! Squawk! Hiss!*
                    *Morning!*

*Nightfall!*

The moon rose like a shimmering silver orb,
Gliding across the gods' pool table,
Darkness creeps like a devil's curse,
Covering the land in an eerie silence,
Nocturnal creatures roam like kings,
Waiting for a feast of fun!
*Rustle! Crack! Argh!*
                    *Nightfall!*

**Hannah Ingham  (10)**
**Rattray Primary School, Rattray**

# Rainforest

*Morning!*

The sun rose like a yellow tennis ball
Floating over the Amazon's rainforest
Rain drips like balls of ice
Slashing on the lazing leopards
Steam rises like hissing snakes
Disguising the angry crocodile
Awakening the sleeping eagle. *Squawk!*

*Nightfall*

The moon rises like a lonely tear
Drifting across the cute fruit bats
Darkness creeps like a black shadow
Covering the lazy sloths
Nocturnal creatures crawl like wiggly worms
Waiting to ambush a prey! *Roar*
*Nightfall.*

**Gregor Thomas  (9)**
**Rattray Primary School, Rattray**


# Rainforest Rainbow

Red is the colour of an anaconda's flickering tongue
Orange is the colour of the tiger's eyes
Yellow is the colour of the toucan's beak
Green is the colour of the poisonous frogs
Blue is the colour of the thick blue sky
Indigo is the colour of the butterflies' wings flapping in the sun
Violet is the colour of the macaws' wings with other colours.

**Sarah Small  (10)**
**Rattray Primary School, Rattray**

# My Friend

*(Inspired by 'The writer of this Poem' by Roger McGough)*

My very funny friend is,
As silly as a clown,
As cool as a cucumber,
As royal as a crown.

As lively as a puppy,
As impatient as a clock,
As loud as a drum roll,
As ticky as a tock.

As wise as an owl,
As chatty as a box,
As hungry as a yum-yum,
As sneaky as a fox.

As clumsy as an elephant,
As fizzy as Coke,
And my funny friend, I hope,
Knows how to take a joke!

**Laura Clegg  (11)**
**St Dominic's RC Primary School, Crieff**


# The Zoo

In the zoo the animals rule,
The monkeys moan,
The lions dance,
The hippos bathe in the water,

The giraffes stretch and stretch,
The penguins never stop eating,
The bears just get fluffier,
Then the zookeeper comes

Right lunchtime!

Munching, gobbling, crunching, chomping, scoffing!

**Merissa De Lange  (11)**
**St Dominic's RC Primary School, Crieff**

# Frosty Morning In The Playground

It's a cold frosty morning
On the cold frosty ground.
There are birds whistling
Through the cold, shivery sky.

As the trees breezed in the frosty wind
Snow melting like an ice cream cone
Snowballs smashing against windows and walls
The sun sparkling like the moon in the night sky.

People screaming and laughing like hyenas
on the African plains.
People running like mad scientists when they do
something exciting.

The trees rustling and rumbling in the frosty breeze
It's a cold and frosty morning
In the cold and frosty playground.

**Ashley O'Neill (11)**
**St Dominic's RC Primary School, Crieff**


# What Am I?

What am I?
I am as heavy as a brick,
As grey as rain clouds,
Flying through the air.

I'm as boring as a mouse,
But as loud as a lion.
I'm as strong as a crane,
And I'm as big as a house.

I like to see people,
But not too often.
Have you guessed yet?
What am I?

**Christopher Bendall (11)**
**St Dominic's RC Primary School, Crieff**

# Breakdowns

I was driving along the forest path,
Axe in boot, trailer attached,
When I heard a tree's evil wrath,
Yelling at my car which shouted back.

The tree yelled in an old wooden voice,
'I just cleaned that air,'
The car replied in a well oiled voice,
'That doesn't matter 'cause I don't care.'

'You dirty root down so low,'
Was the answer to this,
As a branch came through the window,
I jumped in fear and screamed at this.

The bonnet flew up roaring with rage,
The engine exposed itself almost sick,
Fuming and sparkling said, as if in a cage,
'You'll pay for that one you old stick.'

Out of the car I ran and ran,
Just in time, for the tree started
Launching leaves to the engine, making it jam,
And I am now very cowardly hearted!

**Callum Anderson  (11)**
**St Dominic's RC Primary School, Crieff**


# Dragons

D ragons, gliding above their prey
R eady to strike it down
A ching to roast its tender flesh
G reat talons glinting in the gloom
O range eyes viewing the plains
N ight envelops their territory in blackness
S cales sparkling like shining death, as they dive towards their prey.

**Benedict Robinson  (11)**
**St Dominic's RC Primary School, Crieff**

# The Secret Life Of Teachers

Have you ever wondered
What teachers do,
When they have days off
Or when they go to the loo?

They're secret agents
That stop petty-theft,
If they carry on
There'll be no villains left!

They could be aliens
From outer space,
Come to our school
To invade the place.

They're superheroes
That save the land,
Their gold cape flies
As they lend a hand.

But I guess we'll have to keep wondering
What teachers do,
When they have days off
Or when they go to the loo?

**Morven McGuigan  (11)**
**St Dominic's RC Primary School, Crieff**

# Haunted?

A tall black gate,
A creepy door,
A haunted house?
Rats on the floor.

A screaming noise,
Where? Over there?
Don't really know,
Don't really care.

Through the small door,
In the next room,
Could possibly be,
In the house of doom.

A screaming noise,
Where? Over there?
Don't really know,
Don't really care.

I can hear a noise,
Coming from the tower.
I think it might just be,
The evil witch's power.

**Charlotte Macdonald  (11)**
**St Dominic's RC Primary School, Crieff**

# The Fairground

When we get in I shout hooray
Running, jumping and dancing.
My little sister wants to play,
Gaping at everything!

Let's go on the roller coaster, I say,
OK they agree,
Queuing up takes so long,
But gets fun when it's our turn.

We go up and down,
Spinning round and round,
I scream and shout,
Laughing round and about!

Then we have lunch at a hot dog stall
With smells wafting out,
We sit down and eat,
Watching people busy about.

'I want to go on the log flumes,'
Alice screams and shouts.
'they're cool, wet and wonderful,' Dad agrees
'Yippee! Whee!'

Frank's dying for the ghost train,
Dad takes him. Seeing ghosts
Makes me shiver
The ghost train is the one I hate the most.

Now it's time to go home.

**Kirsty Maclean (10)**
**St Dominic's RC Primary School, Crieff**

# The Suffering Forest

Oh the forest,
Oh the forest,
How I love the forest,
With the beauty of the trees.

They come with fire,
They come with axes,
The trees must make a stand,
Join together in unity.

Attack with stones,
Defend with branches,
Stand in victory,
And watch your enemies flee.

Oh the forest,
Oh the forest,
How they need the forest.
Hasn't the forest suffered enough?

**Michael Addley  (11)**
**St Dominic's RC Primary School, Crieff**


# Poverty

P overty is ruining innocent people's lives
O ver the world people suffer
V ictims of disaster
E very one of them is starving
R eally ill people running out of food with no medical treatment
T oo many are dying with no help, but
Y ou could change all this.

**Roslyn Ward  (11)**
**St Dominic's RC Primary School, Crieff**

# Rainy Scotland

I woke up this morning,
Feeling tired!
I looked out the window!
And I was inspired!
Because it was raining.

Now it was sunny,
And people were walking around with no tops on.
I thought it was funny.
Because it started to hailstone.

It was now nearly night,
And I was very tired.
After this rainy horrible day,
When I was nearly fired.

**Bobby Garforth (11)**
**St Dominic's RC Primary School, Crieff**


# Roller Coaster

Why, oh why does
The roller coaster run?
It is so scary,
And also so much fun.

Why, oh why does
The roller coaster curve?
It is exciting,
But it will break a nerve.

Why, oh why does
The roller coaster loop?
It is so twisty,
It's sure to have a scoop!

**Eliot Johnstone (11)**
**St Dominic's RC Primary School, Crieff**

## There's Something New In The Playground

There's something new in the playground,
But there's so much noise I can't think,
I think that something's different,
I feel that something's changed.

Everyone looks suspicious,
Everyone's crowding round,
No one's even told me,
There's something fun in the ground.

I'm starting to get the picture,
I've really missed something out,
Something really exciting,
Something in and out!

**Hannah McAuley  (11)**
**St Dominic's RC Primary School, Crieff**

# Skating

Skating is so much fun
Because you don't have to run.

Skating is exciting
But it can also be frightening.

Skating is a blast
Because you can go real fast.

Skating is hard to do
While you shout yahoo!

Skating is so rad
When you're feeling kind of sad.

**Joel Welch  (11)**
**St Dominic's RC Primary School, Crieff**

# Poverty!

M ake poverty history
A lot of the world is in poverty
K illing large amounts
E xtreme poverty over the world

P eople are dying
O nly we can save them
V iolence won't save them
E very three seconds children die of poverty
R eally desperate
T ired and starved
Y es, it's all bad

H ungry and needy
I wish we could do more
S itting on the hard ground
T oday is the day to help
O we them all you can
R eady to save them
Y ou can help.

**Jessica Wake  (11)**
**St Dominic's RC Primary School, Crieff**


# Arctic Fox

The long summer days start to draw in.
My coat changes colour.
The winter turns my coat pure white.
My body is petite.
I have a diminutive face.
My tail is like a white feather duster.
That's why I think
I'm the best looking animal
In the world.

**Louise Pickthall  (11)**
**St Peter's RC Primary School, Dalbeattie**

# The Gharial

Its narrow snout
Hides in the sand.
His jaws open and
*Snap.*

The blood runs
Down into the
Sandy red water.

He slithers out to sea,
Then returns unexpectedly
Traps, snaps, crunch!
More blood.

His teeth clench together.
Feathers floating in the water.
Waves bringing them to shore.
Then, he quietly departs.

**Chanice McLean  (11)**
**St Peter's RC Primary School, Dalbeattie**


# The Bengal Tiger

The strong, vigorous tiger
Has big yellow eyes,
Glowing in the dark.
He hunts stealthily,
Then pounces on his prey.
Kills creatures twice his size.
With his big sharp teeth
He massacres another buffalo.
He is supreme
Above other animals.
He rips at the flesh
Until the victim dies,
Buries it with leaves
And comes back for it later.

**Ashlie Broll  (12)**
**St Peter's RC Primary School, Dalbeattie**

# The Grey Wolf

The grey wolf,
Howls all night,
At the full moon.

Attacks on humans are rare,
I suppose that's fair,
Not one predator,
Attacks the grey wolf.
They grey wolf will feast,
Like a beast on fish, deer and fox,
Its teeth are normally bloody teeth.

Its vision is good for food.
The grey wolf can outrun
Numerous species of animals.

The largest member of the dog family,
Lives happily with his dog offspring,
This is an animal that you need to treat with respect.

**Fraser Drummond  (11)**
**St Peter's RC Primary School, Dalbeattie**

# A Barn Owl's Night Hunting

Tyto alba swoops down from the rafters.
A night's hunting begins.

She soars over the forest.
A helpless mouse is sighted.

The target is made.
The poor mammal,
Doesn't stand a chance.

She swoops down.
Silent as the grave.

The attack is executed.
Poor mouse,
It squeals.
Tries to run, but in vain.

She snatches up her prey in her talons
And swoops off.

A night's hunting is over.

**Fraser Gray  (9)**
**St Peter's RC Primary School, Dalbeattie**

# The Harvest Mouse

Her life is short.
Too short.
As she creeps in the field,
Darkness falls.
The vulnerable thing,
Darts to the seeds.
She disappears in amongst the wheat.
Only two months left.
Then . . .
She's gone.

Seeds and fruit she eats.
She hunts every day.
Only her left in her family.
She will be going next.
Only one month left.
Then . . .
She's gone.

She chases her tail for fun.
But then, she gets bored.
She finds a berry.
She saves it for the next day.
Not long to go now.
She goes to her nest to rest and falls asleep.
The next day she's *dead*.

She's gone now.
What can anybody do?
There she lies in a bundle of wheat.
There will be no going back.
She's gone.

**Rhianna Rae  (10)**
**St Peter's RC Primary School, Dalbeattie**

# The Cheetah

There she was
Sitting in the long grass,
Camouflaged, sitting, waiting
For something to appear.

She started to get anxious
It was quiet, too quiet.
She started to get uncomfortable,
Sitting in the sun.

She strode through the long grass,
Her soft, padded paws faintly touched the ground,
Her eyes started to darken,
Into a shade of black.

She curled up under a dead tree trunk.
She buried her head into her spotted fur.
She closed her eyes
And fell asleep.

She whipped her eyes open,
As quick as a flash.
The painful noise of a gun,
Repeated through her head.

She quickly sat up and scanned the area.
She looked above her head,
The bullet smoke, still in view.
She followed the line to spot the hunter.

Trying to hide, he took another shot.
But she was too fast.
She sprinted into the bush.
The gun was no match for her.

**Mhairi Valentine (10)**
**St Peter's RC Primary School, Dalbeattie**

# Why Vandalise?

People vandalise because
They think it is fun.

People vandalise because
They think they're smart.

People vandalise because
They're jealous.

People vandalise because
They are angry.

People vandalise because
They had to do a dare.

People vandalise because
They think their friends will like them more.

People vandalise because
They're taking revenge.

People vandalise because
Of drugs.

People vandalise because
Of drink.

People vandalise because
They're bored.

People vandalise because
They just don't think, so they do it for nothing.

**Danielle McIntosh  (10)**
**Saline Primary School, Saline**

# Why Vandalise?

Why vandalise when you can have so much fun?
Wouldn't you like to play in the sun
Or is it a dare
That isn't fair?
Why do you still do it?

Maybe it's because you're so bored
Maybe it's because you want to vandalise
A Ford
Why do it if you get in trouble?
Why do it if you make it double?

Why be so cruel?
If you don't get to rule
Why do you spray?
If you have to pay
Why do you still do it?

**Calum Leask  (11)**
**Saline Primary School, Saline**


# Why Vandalise?

Why vandalise?
Because they have nothing to do.

We need to do something to stop them.

What?
Give them things to do.

Who can it be?
Boys and girls from high school.

But CCTV should sort them out.

But why vandalise if there is no prize, nothing?

**Eilidh Moyes  (11)**
**Saline Primary School, Saline**

# Why Vandalise?

Stop, stop, don't vandalise?
Don't destroy you big, bad boy!
Stop, think it's up to you,
Don't vandalise and you'll feel very good!
So don't, don't vandalise, 'cause you
Don't get a prize.
You don't trust, you don't gain pride!

Stop, stop, think it's up to you
Don't vandalise and you'll feel very good!
Girls, girls, why vandalise when you
Don't get a prize!
You may take drugs, you may drink wine,
But you'll end up paying a fine!
Oh yeah!

**Sophie Jeffrey  (10)**
**Saline Primary School, Saline**


# Why Vandalise?

V andals destroy
A ngry vandals spray everything in sight
N othing is safe when vandals are about
D efiant vandals will take revenge
A lcohol makes people break things
L ying vandals don't get away
I f a vandal is grumpy, he/she will have a laugh
S o be prepared
E ggs are thrown by vandals.

**Alex Monk  (11)**
**Saline Primary School, Saline**

## Why Vandalise?

Vandals are not cool, they're just fools.
They may think they're smart but they have no heart.
After they drink, they need to think,
Why take drugs, it only turns you into thugs?
Neds may think they rule, they're all just cruel.
One more crime and it won't be fine.
Stop what you do, it's all up to you.
Just think, just think.
Acting all big, man will make you lose your friends man,
People vandalise because they think it's cool,
People vandalise because they think they rule,
So stop what you do, it's all up to you,
Just think, just think.

**Robbie Gordon (11)**
**Saline Primary School, Saline**


## Vandalise

V andalism is caused by
A nger
N astiness
D efiance
A ttacking
L ying
I n the streets, bored and stressed
S mashing bottles
E very day and every night.

**Lewis Kerr (11)**
**Saline Primary School, Saline**

# Why Vandalise?

People vandalise because they think it's cool.
People vandalise because they think they rule.
People vandalise because they think it's smart.
People vandalise because they think they are stars.
People vandalise because they think they are going too far.
People vandalise because they think they are getting respect.
People vandalise because they think they are boring people.
People vandalise because they think it's cool.
People vandalise because they think they rule!

**Sean Sutherland  (11)**
**Saline Primary School, Saline**


# Why Vandalise?

Why vandalise if there's no watching eyes?
Why vandalise if there's no real prize?
Why vandalise if people think it's lies?

If you vandalise it will be with you forever,
It will vandalise you,
It will cause an unhealable scar.

That one moment,
When it all happened,
That one moment when you could have stopped,
That one moment when your mind popped.

**Ryan Watson  (11)**
**Saline Primary School, Saline**

## Why Vandalise?

Why, why vandalise?
It's bad to do and it's up to you.
So why? Why make a mess?
There's not much point, so give it a rest.
So why? Why vandalise?
There's not much point, it's just not right.
Why vandalise?
It just gets you in trouble and you could get fined.
Why vandalise?
It may sound fun, but it shouldn't be done
And it does not rule and it's not that cool.

**Aimee Aird (11)**
**Saline Primary School, Saline**


## Why Vandalise?

Who are vandals?
What do they do?
Vandals are people who are so cruel,
All vandals do is make up rules,
They think they're cool!
But really they just drool!
Why vandalise if it's not cool,
They get bored so they spray on walls,
They should pay if they spray,
They're just fools if vandals think they rule.

**Joe Butler (11)**
**Saline Primary School, Saline**

# Why Vandalise?

One night I saw three boys on a doorstep.
They had tins of paint in their hands.
Then at that moment I saw the worst thing anyone could do
And guess what they did?
They painted their name on someone else's steps.
And then I thought, *why vandalise?*
Because they don't get anything good or cool.
All they get is into trouble and probably have to pay a fine.
And that's what happened on that very night
I looked out of my window.

**Kenna Grantham  (11)**
**Saline Primary School, Saline**


# Happiness

Happiness is minty-green,
The sea on a sunny day,
The smell of fresh pineapple,
Happiness sounds like the salty sea,
The gentle touch of silky fabric,
The taste of chocolate melting in your mouth,
Happiness is great.

**Rebekah Wallace  (9)**
**Stanley Primary School, Ardrossan**


# Happiness Is ...

Happiness is a sparkling gold,
A sky full of white fluffy clouds,
The smell of freshly picked roses,
The sound of birds twittering far away,
The touch of soft cotton wool,
The taste of sweet, watery melon.
Happiness is just magical.

**Kimberly Pringle  (9)**
**Stanley Primary School, Ardrossan**

# Happiness

Happiness is like bright orange,
Dolphins jumping out of the lovely blue sea,
The smell of fresh air when you go out and play,
The sound of birds singing in the morning,
Happiness is like the soft and smooth feel of velvet,
The taste of nice, juicy green apples in the garden,
Happiness is absolutely wonderful.

**Sarah-Jane Howie (8)**
**Stanley Primary School, Ardrossan**


# Happiness

Happiness is bright gold,
A beautiful green tree growing juicy green apples,
The lovely smell of peach air freshener,
The sound of the colourful busy bees in the morning,
The rough touch of colourful carpets,
Happiness is full of magic things.

**Lee McIntosh (8)**
**Stanley Primary School, Ardrossan**


# Happiness

Happiness is rich red,
A sunset in the evening,
The smell of red, sour strawberries,
The sound of the birds in the morning,
Happiness is the touch of smooth velvet,
The taste of the fruits in the garden,
Happiness is wonderful.

**Jordan Gray (9)**
**Stanley Primary School, Ardrossan**

# Playgrounds, Playgrounds, Playgrounds

Scoobie playgrounds,
Painted playgrounds,
Bouncy, groovy, funky playgrounds,
Grassy, empty, spacious playgrounds,
Those are just a few.

Infant playgrounds,
Fun playgrounds,
Bullying, dull, rough playgrounds,
Bumpy, friendly, small playgrounds,
Active, cool too.

Concrete playgrounds,
Big playgrounds,
Modern, Victorian, grey playgrounds,
Last of all, best of all,
I like sporty playgrounds.

**Mark Coyle  (10)**
**Stanley Primary School, Ardrossan**


# Playgrounds, Playgrounds, Playgrounds

Cool playgrounds,
Funky playgrounds,
Fun, colourful, friendly playgrounds,
Grassy, groovy, spacious playgrounds,
Those are just a few.

Big playgrounds,
Small playgrounds,
Smooth, grey, concrete playgrounds,
Bully, scary, Victorian playgrounds,
Haunted playgrounds too.

Infant playgrounds,
Senior playgrounds,
Environmental friendly playgrounds,
Last of all, best of all,
I like Stanley's playgrounds.

**Kirsty Skene  (10)**
**Stanley Primary School, Ardrossan**

# Houses! Houses! Houses!

Scary houses,
Haunted houses,
Footballers, rich, fancy houses,
Big fat king's houses,
Those are just a few.

Chocolate houses,
Sweet houses,
Big fat scary houses,
Poor brown muddy houses,
Large houses too.

Strawberry houses,
Wendy houses,
Don't forget the tree houses,
Last of all, best of all,
I like ice houses.

**Rebekka Muir (9)**
**Stanley Primary School, Ardrossan**


# Houses! Houses! Houses!

Snobby houses,
Haunted houses,
Wee, thingy majieger houses,
Crocked, wiggly wobbly houses,
Those are just a few.

Stupid houses,
Silly houses,
Melted chocolate treacle houses,
Straw, silk, soft houses,
I like too.

Tree houses,
Paper houses,
Don't forget the town houses,
Last of all, best of all,
I like luxurious houses!

**Kerkyra Kantas Davis (10)**
**Stanley Primary School, Ardrossan**

# Playgrounds, Playgrounds, Playgrounds

Big playgrounds,
Small playgrounds,
Grassy, sporty, active playgrounds,
Fun, spacious, busy playgrounds,
Those are just a few.

Rough playgrounds,
Smooth playgrounds,
Empty, bullying littered playgrounds,
Dull, grey, dark playgrounds,
Modern playgrounds too.

Infant playgrounds,
Junior playgrounds,
Don't forget senior playgrounds,
Last of all, best of all,
I like Stanley's playground.

**Nicola Hind  (9)**
**Stanley Primary School, Ardrossan**


# Houses! Houses! Houses!

Big houses,
Little houses,
Poor, muddy brown houses,
Tall tree boy houses,
Those are just a few.

Demolished houses,
Stone houses,
Stitched, silk, cotton houses
Coffee cappuccino houses
Gran's house too.

Fat houses,
Army houses,
Skinny, holiday, chalet houses,
Last of all, best of all
I like my house.

**Jordan Watt  (9)**
**Stanley Primary School, Ardrossan**

# Playgrounds, Playgrounds, Playgrounds

Dull playgrounds,
Grey playgrounds,
Old, littered, bullying playgrounds,
Haunted, old, scary playgrounds,
Those are just a few.

Big playgrounds,
Small playgrounds,
Fun, grassy, spacious playgrounds,
Spacious, big, bouncy playgrounds,
Groovy playgrounds too.

Scoobie playgrounds,
String playgrounds,
Big, string, Scoobie playgrounds,
Last of all, best of all,
I like Stanley's playgrounds.

**Ashleigh Myers (9)**
**Stanley Primary School, Ardrossan**

# Playground, Playground, Playground

Funky playgrounds,
Groovy playgrounds,
Bouncy, colourful, cool playgrounds,
Spacious, big, smooth playgrounds,
Those are just a few.

Victorian playgrounds,
Modern playgrounds,
Rough, eco, small playgrounds,
Grassy, football, friendly playgrounds,
Haunted ones too.

Fun playgrounds,
Dull playgrounds,
Concrete Stanley, busy playgrounds,
Last of all, best of all,
I like *spooky* playgrounds.

**Sarah-Jayne Meek (10)**
**Stanley Primary School, Ardrossan**

# Playgrounds, Playgrounds, Playgrounds

Dull playgrounds,
Modern playgrounds,
Smooth, small, sporty playgrounds,
Active, spacious, grassy playgrounds,
Those are just a few.

Bright playgrounds,
Colourful playgrounds,
Computer, wasp free playgrounds,
Spider, girl free playgrounds,
Concrete grey too.

Funky playgrounds,
Groovy playgrounds,
Infant, junior, senior playgrounds,
Last of all, best of all,
I like Stanley playgrounds.

**Gordon Wallace (9)**
**Stanley Primary School, Ardrossan**


# Playgrounds, Playgrounds, Playgrounds

Bumpy playgrounds,
Funky playgrounds,
Big, bouncy, bright playgrounds,
Spacious, smooth, small playgrounds,
Those are just a few.

Cool playgrounds,
Concrete playgrounds,
Fun, friendly, football playgrounds,
Green, grassy, groovy playgrounds,
Bully free too.

Littered playgrounds,
Lovely playgrounds,
Scary, haunted, grey playgrounds,
Last of all, best of all,
I like playful playgrounds.

**Matthew Duff (9)**
**Stanley Primary School, Ardrossan**

## Playground, Playground, Playground

Dull playgrounds,
Small playgrounds,
Rough, grey, bumpy playgrounds,
Victorian, modern, bullying,
Those are just a few.

Active playgrounds,
Groovy playgrounds,
Funky, cool, busy playgrounds,
Colourful, fun, big playgrounds,
Stanley playgrounds too.

Friendly playgrounds,
Football playgrounds,
Bouncy, grassy, small playgrounds,
Last of all, best of all,
I like Stanley's playgrounds.

**Aimee Ferguson (9)**
**Stanley Primary School, Ardrossan**


## Playground, Playground, Playground

Funky playgrounds,
Groovy playgrounds,
Grassy, bouncy, fun playgrounds,
Big, smooth, cool playgrounds,
Those are just a few.

Small playgrounds,
Grey playgrounds,
Scoobie, friendly, active playgrounds,
Sad, lonely, still playgrounds,
Happy playgrounds too.

Small playgrounds,
Big playgrounds,
Still, stupid, twisty playgrounds,
Last of all, best of all,
I like Stanley playgrounds.

**Linda Young (9)**
**Stanley Primary School, Ardrossan**

# Playgrounds, Playgrounds, Playgrounds

Haunted playgrounds,
Scary playgrounds,
Tall, small, big playgrounds,
Dull, grey, grassy playgrounds,
Those are just a few.

Football playgrounds,
Scoobie playgrounds,
Littered, smooth, empty playgrounds,
Infant, rainbow, groovy playgrounds,
Fun and friendly too.

Bumpy playgrounds,
Busy playgrounds,
Tough, bouncy, groovy playgrounds,
Last of all, best of all,
I like my playgrounds.

**Connie Bailey  (10)**
**Stanley Primary School, Ardrossan**


# Playground, Playground, Playground

Dull playgrounds,
Bumpy playgrounds,
Bullying playgrounds,
Empty, scary, haunted playgrounds,
Those are just a few.

Nice playgrounds,
Friendly playgrounds,
Groovy, funky, spacious playgrounds,
Grassy, big, football playgrounds,
Cool playgrounds too.

Empty playgrounds,
Grey playgrounds,
Small, bumpy, bouncy playgrounds,
Last of all, best of all,
I like colourful playgrounds.

**Alexander MacLaren  (10)**
**Stanley Primary School, Ardrossan**

# Playgrounds, Playgrounds, Playgrounds

Active playgrounds,
Big playgrounds,
Smooth, damp, cold playgrounds,
Empty, small, busy playgrounds,
Those are just a few.

Bouncy playgrounds,
Litter playgrounds,
Hard, rough, smooth playgrounds,
Grassy, concrete, cool playgrounds,
Bully free too.

Groovy playgrounds,
Funky playgrounds,
Bully, bumpy, dull playgrounds,
Last of all, best of all,
I like Stanley's playground.

**Craig Munn (10)**
**Stanley Primary School, Ardrossan**

# Playgrounds, Playgrounds, Playgrounds

Bumpy playgrounds,
Concrete playgrounds,
Groovy, funky, friendly playgrounds,
Colourful, playful, helpful playgrounds,
Those are just a few.

Grassy playgrounds,
Bouncy playgrounds,
Fun, dull, empty playgrounds,
Busy, modern too.

Cool playgrounds,
Fun playgrounds,
Smooth, small, grey playgrounds,
Last of all, best of all,
I like classic playgrounds.

**Paige Russell (9)**
**Stanley Primary School, Ardrossan**

## Happiness

Happiness is shiny silver like stars in the night sky,
The smell of chocolate fudge cake,
The sound of birds singing in the morning,
Happiness is the touch of a new leather suite,
The taste of a melt in your mouth ice cream.
Happiness is magical!

**Gavin Lundy (9)**
**Stanley Primary School, Ardrossan**


## Happiness

Happiness is the colour of the sunset,
A black pony with a white star,
The smell of juicy sweet, ripe strawberries,
The sound of a clarinet playing in the distance,
The touch of a smooth horse,
The taste of chocolate mice,
Happiness is a joy.

**Jena Montgomerie (8)**
**Stanley Primary School, Ardrossan**


## Happiness

Happiness is dark blue
A sky dotted with shiny, sparkling stars
The smell of fresh baked pies are in the air
The sound of a music box in the morning
Happiness is a soft, smooth touch of silk
The taste of ripe plums in the fruit bowl
Happiness is wonderful!

**Lisa Barraclough (8)**
**Stanley Primary School, Ardrossan**

# Happiness

Happiness is summery yellow
A playground full of people getting on with each other
The smell of red, rosy, fresh apples
The sound of the wind whistling in the night
The very smooth touch of cotton wool
Happiness is the taste of fish and chips
Happiness is magic.

**Marcus McCrindle (9)**
**Stanley Primary School, Ardrossan**


# Happiness

Happiness is a summery yellow
A sky with all kinds of birds
The smell of fresh bananas
The sound of joy and laughter of children outdoors
Happiness is the touch of a new baby's smooth hair
The taste of tropical ripe fruits in the garden
Happiness is wonderful in many ways!

**Danielle Gilmour (8)**
**Stanley Primary School, Ardrossan**


# Happiness

Happiness is bright orange,
A sky dotted with fluffy clouds,
The delightful smell of roses in the garden,
The sound of the birds singing in the afternoon,
Happiness is the smooth touch of velvet,
The taste of milk chocolate,
Happiness is magnificent.

**Rachael McMullan (9)**
**Stanley Primary School, Ardrossan**

# Happiness

Happiness is shiny yellow
A sky shaped with big black birds
The smell of cherry-red small flowers
A sound of the wavy, light blue sea
Happiness is the hot, smooth and soft cushion
The juicy taste of bright yellow pineapple
Happiness is joyful and fun.

**Alannah Bailey (9)**
**Stanley Primary School, Ardrossan**


# Happiness

Happiness is light pink
The river is crowded with swans
The smell of juicy green pears
The sound of birds tweeting
The touch of soft velvet
The taste of juicy green grapes
Happiness is wonderful, cheerful, joyful.

**Lauren Lynch (9)**
**Stanley Primary School, Ardrossan**


# Happiness

Happiness is Baby bell pink,
I see a butterfly with dotted spots,
The smell of rosy flowers,
I hear my dog in the morning,
Happiness is to touch the new furry carpet,
The taste of Mars Delight chocolate,
Happiness is beautiful.

**Georgie McDougall (8)**
**Stanley Primary School, Ardrossan**

# Happiness

Happiness is as green as the grass in the meadow
The smell of the flowers in the flower bed
The sound of the owl waking in the night
Happiness is a nice touch of a new carpet
The taste of a big juicy pear
Happiness is the best feeling.

**Rachel Blades  (8)**
**Stanley Primary School, Ardrossan**


# Happiness

Happiness is like the lovely blue sea,
A sky filled with fluffy white clouds,
The smell of lovely red roses,
The sound of peace and quiet at night,
Happiness is the smooth touch of soft leather.
Happiness is sour raspberries.
Happiness is a great wonderful thing!

**Drue Lauren Brown  (9)**
**Stanley Primary School, Ardrossan**


# Happiness

Happiness is a black sky
Happiness is tired seagulls in the sky
I like the smell of chicken
I like to hear the car exhaust going
I like to touch the school pencil
I like the taste of chicken
Happiness is football.

**Jonathan Muir  (8)**
**Stanley Primary School, Ardrossan**

# Happiness

Happiness is bright red
Like watching the football on TV
I like to smell oil
I like to hear the singing on TV
I like to touch soft things
I like to taste mint
Happiness is full of hope.

**Shaun Jackson  (8)**
**Stanley Primary School, Ardrossan**


# Happiness

Happiness is lovely baby pink,
A sky full of fluffy clouds,
The smell of juicy red apples,
The nice touch of silk,
The noise of singing,
The taste of tropical orange.
Happiness is joyful.

**Carly Morris  (8)**
**Stanley Primary School, Ardrossan**


# Happiness

Happiness is dark blue
Football players passing the ball
The smell of ripe fruit
The sound of children laughing
Happiness is the touch of a fluffy dog
The taste of lovely hot doughnuts
Happiness is a great feeling.

**Craig Mackay  (9)**
**Stanley Primary School, Ardrossan**

# Playgrounds, Playgrounds, Playgrounds

Dull playgrounds,
Grey playgrounds,
Old, little, boring playgrounds,
Sad, crying, empty playgrounds,
Those are just a few.

Bright playgrounds,
Colourful playgrounds,
Happy, bully free playgrounds,
Environmental, friendly playgrounds,
Fun playgrounds too.

Winton's playgrounds,
St Peter's playgrounds,
Glasgow's Springburn Primary playgrounds,
Last of all, best of all,
I like Stanley's playgrounds.

**Emma Steven (10)**
**Stanley Primary School, Ardrossan**


# Playgrounds, Playgrounds, Playgrounds

Fun playgrounds,
Colourful playgrounds,
Fair, sport, football playgrounds,
Big, smooth, Stanley playgrounds,
Those are just a few.

Grassy playgrounds,
Bullying playgrounds,
Litter, free, grey playgrounds,
Friendly, bumpy, small playgrounds,
Empty, busy playgrounds too.

Cool playgrounds,
Groovy playgrounds,
Modern, eco, funky playgrounds,
Last of all, best of all,
I like haunted playgrounds.

**Nathan Lee Wieringa (9)**
**Stanley Primary School, Ardrossan**

# Playgrounds, Playgrounds, Playgrounds

Old playgrounds,
Haunted playgrounds,
Busy, bad, nasty playgrounds,
Rough, empty, dull playgrounds,
Those are just a few.

Active playgrounds,
Cool playgrounds,
Groovy, funky, friendly playgrounds,
Spacious, grassy, colourful playgrounds,
Bumpy playgrounds too.

Ornamental playgrounds,
Still playgrounds,
Happy, wild, bright playgrounds,
Clean, tidy, grey playgrounds,
Last of all, best of all,
I like quiet playgrounds.

**Gemma Dunlop (10)**
**Stanley Primary School, Ardrossan**


# Scolty Wood In Autumn

It was cold and windy
I wore my woolly scarf
I closed the door
Leaves swirled around my feet.

There is a creeping
And a leaping
Leaves were swirling, twirling, burring
All around my feet.

Crimson, red, copper, bronze
Rusty, crusty, mustard, custard,
The leaves of autumn.

**Sarah Middleton (11)**
**Strachan Primary School, Banchory**

# Autumn Tongue Twister

It's autumn!
Time to get your tongue working
This will certainly get your tongue
Twisting and turning
For this is the tongue twister of autumn -
Crispy, crunchy, creepy, crowded
(Don't go now we are just getting started)
Crunchy, rustling, crumbly, hustling
Bumpy, wrinkly rug.
Red and scarlet
Brown and rusty
All rise up,
The wind is gusty,
Orange, copper, bronzy, yellow
Charcoal black and minty yellow.

**Oliver Middleton  (8)**
**Strachan Primary School, Banchory**


# Autumn Sounds

I stand at the window
Leaves are blowing in the gale
In a minute that crimson one
Will probably set sail.
I go outside - the grass has gone
A carpet has been laid
As red as berries
As amber as a necklace
As brown as chocolate cake
As orange as a tangerine
As green as mint
As yellow as mustard.
I will always love that multicoloured carpet.

**Joanne Stewart  (9)**
**Strachan Primary School, Banchory**

# Crow's Wood

It was a cold, cold wintry night
In Crow's Wood the leaves waved from side to side,
All night crows squawked,
All night leaves floated in the air
Someone crept through the creepy wood
Leaves drifted to the forest floor forming a doormat.
The man's face was like a russet leaf
His body was as cold as a polar bear's nose
Leaves crunched and crackled
An old oak tree cackled
The man was glad to be gone.

**Ryan Neish (11)**
**Strachan Primary School, Banchory**


# Last Year In Autumn

Last year I went out to play
My friends and I started to kick the leaves
We walked on the crispy crackly leaves
Then we started to climb trees
We sang, leaves are green and leaves are yellow
And we drank cocoa while singing he's a jolly good fellow.

**Cameron Randalls (10)**
**Strachan Primary School, Banchory**


# Autumn Colours

While walking in the park today
I saw a leaf along the way
It was browny and crusty
Crunchy and rusty
But it was still a leaf.

**Beatrice Reader (9)**
**Strachan Primary School, Banchory**

# Autumn

On the ground a carpet of crimson lies -
A bed of leaves
Crunchingly I walk over it.
It looks like my bed when I get up in the morning.
Under the duvet, some little bugs sit
I walk and I walk,
Until I emerge from the woods.
Then into the sun, leaving the bedroom behind.

**Robert Stroud  (11)**
**Strachan Primary School, Banchory**

# Lost Leaf

I glanced out of the window
And spied the autumn leaves
I ran into the garden
And looked down at my feet,
On the ground was a crusty crimson leaf
Suddenly the wind picked up
I lost my crusty crimson leaf.

**Amy Balfour  (10)**
**Strachan Primary School, Banchory**

# Autumn Sounds

The rustling, crackling along the path
Red, orange and toffee too
Through the air.
I cross the path kicking leaves around
Going bonkers in the woodland.

**Douglas Law  (10)**
**Strachan Primary School, Banchory**

# Autumn

Autumn leaves lie quiet on the ground,
Till suddenly there is a sound,
Three young boys came storming forward,
*Crunch, crunch, crackle, crackle, creak!*

They stomp on the crimson crunching leaves,
Listening for just as long as they please
They jump and laugh and giggle and yell,
*Crunch, crunch, crackle, crackle, creak!*

The three boys run away,
Now I hope it will stay this way,
It is peaceful now the birds have come home
*Crunch, crunch, crackle, crackle, creak!*

**Martha Collier  (10)**
**Strachan Primary School, Banchory**


# Autumn Leaves

As red as a berry,
As brown as a conker,
I kicked up the leaves,
And behaved like a plonker.

**Stuart Gray  (9)**
**Strachan Primary School, Banchory**


# Autumn Colours

In the wood a little dog plays
He scatters the autumnal leaves
He loves chasing flying things
The red, gold and bronze shower
But he never chases the bees.

**Adam Castle  (10)**
**Strachan Primary School, Banchory**

# Night

Night is a black sky
He makes me feel happy
His face looks smiley
His eyes are like a board
His mouth is open
His hair black
His clothes are made of spiders' silk
When he moves he crawls
When he speaks he sways
He lives in a cave with his mother and children
Night is me.

**Lewis Wedderburn  (10)**
**Strathkinness Primary School, Strathkinness**


# Dusk Falls

Yellow eyes like the sunshine,
Hair spiked as a plant growing with colours,
He has a long, sparkly, silk dress,
He moves like the wind in the sky,
He is really tall,
His mouth is an open smile,
He lives in the dark, dark sky,
He has gentle footsteps,
His eyes are open like windows,
Sparkling face like the sky,
He feels like a teddy bear,
He makes me happy, happy as can be,
He speaks quietly as a mouse,
Night is a beautiful person.

**Craig Bayne  (10)**
**Strathkinness Primary School, Strathkinness**

# The Princess Of Dark

I met at dusk the Princess of Dark, her name is powerful
But her soul is kind.
Night has a lovely tanned face, she wears soft make-up
Which shines in moon's light.
Night has sparkling brown eyes.
Her mouth is like a sliver of ice, it never opens.
Her hair is the piece of jigsaw that makes her perfect -
Brown and wavy. Feels like soft sand.
She wears a flowing white gown that blows in the wind.
Night moves slowly and quietly.
She lives at the top of a lovely, green valley in a
White, glittering palace.
Night sings so quietly and softly that she sounds like a bird.
Night makes me think of sweet dreams.
She is lonely but happy.

**Heather Walker  (11)**
**Strathkinness Primary School, Strathkinness**


# The Prince Of Night

At dusk I come out of the heavens,
The Prince of Night.
I glide softly, silently around the starry sky,
Giving children sweet and happy dreams.
My jet-black curly hair and my light black
Cotton clothes blend into the darkness.
I feel peaceful and young.
My small friendly mouth slowly opens
And I start singing, my voice echoing
Around the stars.
As dawn draws near, my soft singing
Voice and my tall elegant body goes
Back to the heavens.
Light returns.

**Joseph Gibbins  (10)**
**Strathkinness Primary School, Strathkinness**

# The Demon Of Darkness

He's sly and quick as he moves
He terrifies from dusk till dawn and then,
Back to his ghostly lair down in the cellars so
Dark, so lonely.

His massive teeth so white, so light
His dark and evil eyes, a demon in the night
A black, ripped, bloodstained wet suit,
A crushed and lonely man.

This murderous being, so nasty.

He moves super fast, his spiky black hair,
He's everywhere, a merciless beast,
So mean, so scary.

**Adam Murray  (11)**
**Strathkinness Primary School, Strathkinness**


# The King Of Sleep

I am the king of sleep,
I am so kind and friendly,
I have blue and white eyes just like the sky,
And a big smile red as a rose,
Long hair as bright as the sun,
I wear a long white cape to guide you into my dreams,
I walk soft and quiet to my house in the wood,
You are so safe in your sweet dreams,
You can hear the twinkling stars and
The moonlight shining down on you,
When you are lying down in comfort.

**Robert Jarvis  (10)**
**Strathkinness Primary School, Strathkinness**

# The Prince Of Night

The Prince of Night has come again,
Sleeping in his shadow he lay,
In his small cottage beyond the sun,
He dreams sweet dreams.

He makes me feel comforting and warm,
When I see him cuddling up snug,
Like a grandpa cuddling me tight,
And wrapping his arms around me.

Hair scruffy like a dog,
Jet-black like the dark sky,
Mangled hair like wires,
Brushes my skin.

He wears a stripy nightgown,
His candle lights up the dark sky,
Being held in his harmless hands
Mouth pursed but always smiling,
Starry and sparkling eyes,
Which shine in the moonlight.

Slowly and elegantly he moves,
Flowing through the fresh clean air,
Hearing the breeze of the winds,
passing through.

The Prince of Night has just passed by,
Sleeping in his shadow he lay
In his small cottage beyond the sun,
He dreams sweet dreams.

**Coral Jackson  (11)**
**Strathkinness Primary School, Strathkinness**

# The Prince Of Darkness

I am the Prince of Darkness,
A villain through and through,
Whenever it is pitch-black,
I come out to get you!

I am always very near,
But also very far,
I am worse than any evil being,
Even worse than Dracula.

My face you cannot see
Because it's hidden under a hood,
You wouldn't want to be with me
When I'm in a bad mood.

My hair is really black,
And my clothes are black too,
My home is on a dark mountain,
And who would want to go there, who?

My voice is really horrible,
It's a voice that could grate cheese,
My mind is full of wicked thoughts
So people please don't tease.

When I move, I'm like a Dalek,
I do not walk but glide,
When anybody sees me coming,
They want to run and hide.

So I am the Prince of Darkness,
A villain through and through,
Now it is pitch-black,
And I'm coming to get yo-o-o-u!

**Alan Sunter (10)**
**Strathkinness Primary School, Strathkinness**

# Count Nightula

It is 8 o'clock and you're nearly asleep,
You think you're safe but you could never be in more danger,
The sun is down and the moon is up,
I have come to get you.
My name is Count Nightula,
Your mother has closed the door and all is dark.
You can feel me coming, advancing upon you
Like a terrorist coming with a nuclear bomb.
People think I comfort you, help you get to sleep.
Oh how wrong they are!
10 o'clock now and your eyes are closed
And you're asleep dreaming.
I move silently across your room, crawl onto
Your bed and dissolve into your head.
My steps are silent as I creep along,
Like a lion closing in on its prey.
I wear a clock of black, with ripped and
Ragged clothes underneath.
My eyes are blood-red with no white at all.
My hair is long, greasy and shaggy.
You see my bright yellow fangs,
You scream as you fall down, down, down, down,
It is 8 o'clock now,
The sun is up and you are safe for now.
But I'll be back soon,
You can count on that.

**Evie Paterson (10)**
**Strathkinness Primary School, Strathkinness**

# The Prince Of Darkness

Watch out for the Prince of Darkness,
He's a very formidable fellow.
He's eerie, he's a complete monster,
He's the Prince of Darkness.

Watch out for his devil horns,
And his tangled hair,
His red, mauve, ruby, evil eyes,
Stare out from his lair.

His swishing cloak makes not a sound,
And as for his weight,
He weighs nothing but a pound,
But he'll still decide your fate.

His only foe is the Prince of Sleep,
But if Darkness gets his way,
He'll transport you to his lair,
Which is Nightmare Bay.

Or he might swoop down on you,
And freeze you to the spot,
You'll stay in that position till,
Dawn comes and you get hot.

Watch out for the Prince of Darkness,
He's a very frightening fellow.
He is eerie; he's a monster,
He's the Prince of Darkness.

**Paul Sinclair  (9)**
**Strathkinness Primary School, Strathkinness**

# The Spirit Of Night

At dawn I walked through the valley of sleep,
I heard his echoey calls.
*The Spirit Of Night* was still awake,
His spell was being called.
He was cursing the sun for blocking him out.
I couldn't hear his footsteps, for he does not walk, he hovers.
His heavy breathing came towards me then I could see his face,
His staring eyes looking straight at me.
His hooked nose was onto my scent; his wrinkly lips,
His short ruffled hair, his long dark cloak.
If you were not too close you could say the hood covered his face.
His cave was by the shadowy pools,
It had gruesome reflections of his face,
If you were used to him, you would know how dangerous
And frightening he was,
He reminds me of horrifying dreams,
Some are his slaves, for they get too close
But I stay in the bushes all alone.

**Callum Barclaywood (9)**
**Strathkinness Primary School, Strathkinness**


# The Princess Of Dusk

As the sun goes down the Princess of Dusk comes out,
She comforts you with her soothing, gentle voice,
A dark silk cloak blowing in the wind.
The princess has a still, loveable face,
With blue staring eyes,
Jet-black hair so silky soft.
As I lie asleep in bed, she moves across me,
Her hair brushing my skin.
When dawn appears she flies back to the clouds.

**Tamara Levy (10)**
**Strathkinness Primary School, Strathkinness**

# Beware As The Sun Goes Down

Beware as the sun goes down for the horror that blocks your path,
He lives in *Demon Lake* where no humans dare to go!
As the dusk casts on the valley, the horror wakes again.
He crawls out of the demoned lake to haunt whom he pleases.
As he seeks to find his prey, he sets his eyes on
Caulder Village where he chooses to haunt once again.
As I lie awake in bed, I hear the door creak,
I feel a cold breath against my cheek and as I turn
My head, two bulging red eyes stare me in the face,
Hundreds of razor teeth.
He lunges with great force and that is the last thing I ever saw!

**Fin Jones (10)**
**Strathkinness Primary School, Strathkinness**


# Princess Of Eve

I met at dusk the beauty of sleep,
Her name was Princess of Eve,
She sings so soft in a harmonious way,
Her clothes so silky and subtle,
Her warming reassuring eyes
make you feel like you're under a spell.
She walks slowly and silently
Through the night,
Her home is in a deserted land
In a soft, floaty, dreamy place.
Rosebud lips are perfectly formed,
Thick, wavy golden-brown hair
Flutters in the wind,
She has you under a spell,
And leaves you for dawn
To awaken you.

**Jennifer Wood (10)**
**Strathkinness Primary School, Strathkinness**

# The Queen Of Sleep

It's night-time now,
The Queen of Sleep will be waking up ready to start her job,
Her smile making you warm and snug,
Her bright red lips and rose perfume lulling you to sleep,
She'll glide over your heads guarding you,
She has bright blue eyes, that can see
For miles for she is the queen of night.
And her job is to send you into happy dreams,
And protect you from the bad ones,
She is like a sister to me and everybody else.

**Lindsey White  (10)**
**Strathkinness Primary School, Strathkinness**


# The Sea

Snarling like an alligator
  searching for its prey,

Rushing like a dog running
  through the swaying grass,

Smashing like a bottle dropping
  from a table

Gurgling like a fish swimming
  quickly away from its enemy

Heaving like a dog dragging
  a heavy branch

And as breathtaking, as graceful swans
  gliding across the moonlight lake

**Shaina Sanderson  (9)**
**Tannadice Primary School, Forfar**

# Me

My cheeks are rosy like a red, juicy apple swaying on the branch,
My teeth are as yellow as the sun newly rising,
My hair is shiny like a pearl glistening on a summer's day,
My eyes are a sapphire-blue as the sky without a cloud in sight,
My lips are rosebud-pink like a rose petal falling swiftly to the grass,
And my nose is as small as a mouse scurrying across the floorboards.

**Anna Kidd (8)**
**Tannadice Primary School, Forfar**


# The Sea

Whipping like the angry tiger's trainer urging him on,
Pounding like a strong, dangerous wind against the glass,
Snapping like a frightening murderer ready to kill,
Snarling like a wild Siberian tiger ready to pounce,
Roaring like an intimidating person so loudly he
                                       wakes everyone up,
And as breathtaking as a newborn kitten,
As cute and as fluffy as can be.

**Alia Kelly (9)**
**Tannadice Primary School, Forfar**


# Me

My hair is as brown as chocolate melted in a bowl,
My eyes are blue like the sea water glistening in the sun,
My eyelashes are as black as a raven's wing,
My cheeks are red like my little sister's hair,
My lips are as small as a robin's feather,
And I am tall like a lamp post lighting up the dark.

**Kirsten Doyle (9)**
**Tannadice Primary School, Forfar**

# The Sea

Gurgling like a car when you put in fuel,
Grinding like the shield when it's just been hit with a sword,
Whipping like cream after it's been whisked,
Pounding like a cat chasing a field mouse,
Smashing like an earthquake attacking a city,
And as intimidating as an angry boxer dog about to knock you down.

**Ryan Farquharson  (10)**
**Tannadice Primary School, Forfar**


# Me

My teeth are as straight as soldiers standing to attention,
My eyes are brown like the bark on a tree,
My head is as hard as cement being made in the mixer,
My lips are red like rosebuds on a cloudless day,
My skin is as smooth as a deer's velvety horn,
And my hair is scruffy like a horse's mane after it's galloped
across the meadow.

**Ruth Moore  (9)**
**Tannadice Primary School, Forfar**


# Me

My lips are as red as the blood dripping from a cut,
My eyes are small like the golden ring on my finger,
My cheeks are as pink as a glowing diamond,
My skin is white like the snowdrops after Christmas,
My eyelashes are as black as a stormy night,
And my hair is wavy like the wheat on a windy day.

**Cheryl Williams  (9)**
**Tannadice Primary School, Forfar**

# Me

My eyes are a mixture of brown and black.
Brown as the hands on the clock saying *tick-tock*.
My hair is straight, like a hundred soldiers standing to attention,
My teeth are as small as my ruler, waiting to be used,
My cheeks are red, like rosy apples about to be crunched,
And my nose is as small as the button on a baby's jumper.

**Alana Edwards (9)**
**Tannadice Primary School, Forfar**

# The Sea

Rushing like the wind in a ferocious storm,
Roaring like a tiger fighting another,
Smashing like a crystal bowl falling from someone's hand,
Crashing like a tree as it hits the ground,
Pounding like someone's heart when they're scared,
And as wild as a cheetah running through the forest.

**Christopher George (9)**
**Tannadice Primary School, Forfar**

# The Sea

Crashing like a telegraph pole tumbling to the ground,
Pounding like a shark about to tear apart its prey,
Rushing like a racing car screeching round the track,
Snapping like a crocodile breaking off a branch,
Grinding like a stone demolishing the wheat,
And as dangerous as a volcano bubbling fire and lava.

**Callum Dunleavy (9)**
**Tannadice Primary School, Forfar**

# Me

My hair is as brown as a chestnut horse galloping through a
                                        secret glade
My eyes are blue like an ocean, where an underwater wonderland lies,
My cheeks are as crimson as the royal cape the Queen wears,
My mouth is like a dark, twisting tunnel, building anxiety,
My teeth are as pearly and straight as granite waiting to be used,
My lips are soft and scarlet like a rose petal blowing in the breeze,
And I am as tall and thin as a willow tree swaying in the wind.

**Molly Wilson  (9)**
**Tannadice Primary School, Forfar**


# Me

My hair is as long and brown as a lion's mane,
My eyelashes are black like the boots on Santa Claus' feet,
My lips are as red as cherries hanging from the tree,
My skin is smooth like the picnic benches at school,
My eyes are as brown as a rabbit hopping in the long grass
And my teeth are as white as a unicorn standing in
                                the gleaming sunlight.

**Emily Baillie  (9)**
**Tannadice Primary School, Forfar**


# The Sea

Smashing like a teenager raging through the house,
Crashing like a puppy dog tugging at the table cloth,
Snarling like a grizzly bear protecting its young,
Pounding like your heart when you see a gun,
Rushing like a waterfall falling from the rocks above,
And as breathtaking as a giant panda
Staring you straight in the face.

**Araminta Yates  (9)**
**Tannadice Primary School, Forfar**

# Me

My teeth are as straight as a soldier marching in a parade,
My hair is brown like a coconut shining in the sunlight,
My lips are as pink as a rose starting to flower,
My pupils are black like the sky at midnight,
My chin is as round as a football spinning in the air
And my eyebrows are dark like the spots on a Dalmatian.

**Gemma Mackintosh (9)**
**Tannadice Primary School, Forfar**


# My Eyes

My eyes are a mixture of blue and grey,
Blue as the sky on the warmest of days,
Blue as the pencils in the pencil box at school,
Blue as a dragonfly's body skimming through the air
And edged with grey
Grey as the armour of a knight,
Grey as the sea on a stormy night.

**Ruth Mayes (9)**
**Tannadice Primary School, Forfar**


# The Sea

Whipping like a cowboy catching a bull,
Smashing like the vase falling to the ground,
Heaving like the slaves dragging the rocks,
Crashing like houses being demolished in the storm,
Pounding like a polar bear breaking through the ice
And as breathtaking as a handful of squirrels
Climbing up the trees.

**Dylan Simpson (10)**
**Tannadice Primary School, Forfar**

# The Sea

Pounding like a kangaroo hopping angrily away,
Crashing like a pussycat running into the wall,
Smashing like my bedroom light falling to the ground,
Snapping like my hair bobble when I pulled it from my hair,
Heaving like a man lifting heavy weights
And as breathtaking as a meadow under the hot sun.

**Megan Barclay (9)**
**Tannadice Primary School, Forfar**


# Me

My ears are as pointy as the Vulcan Spock,
My eyes gleam like the lit-up moon shining down on me,
My hair is as tangled as a thorny rose bush,
My skin is smooth like a glossy pebble on a sandy beach,
My lips are as curved as a perfect circle being drawn
And I am bulky like a brick too strong to be smashed.

**Craig Joiner (9)**
**Tannadice Primary School, Forfar**


# My Eyes

My eyes are a mixture of brown and black,
Brown as the chocolate melting in a bowl,
Brown as the spots on my newborn pups,
Brown as my glossy hair hanging down my back
And hinted with black,
Black as my mum's leather jacket,
Black as the pupil in my eye.

**Laura Herd (9)**
**Tannadice Primary School, Forfar**

# The Sea

Rushing like an ostrich running through the field,
Pounding like a joiner hammering in some nails,
Snapping like a baby breaking plastic toys,
Roaring like a whale diving across the sea,
Crashing like a parent stamping after a child
And as angry as a raging buffalo charging at its enemy.

**John Gibb (10)**
**Tannadice Primary School, Forfar**


# Animals

If I were an animal, I would be a seal,
Small, good at swimming,
Patrycja would be a panda, black and white and cool,
Ishbel would be a dolphin, pretty,
A good diver
Emer would be a cheetah, fast and smart,
Ellie would be a guinea pig, nibbling everything
Dad would be a bird,
He loves them so much.

**Gillean Palmer (7)**
**Tarland Primary School, Tarland**


# Snail

A snail is so slimy and so slow,
I wish I could be a small snail
Slithering everywhere on the land.

**Eilidh Anderson (8)**
**Tarland Primary School, Tarland**

# What Colour Is Pluto?

On a Monday morning,
In the primary school,
Trying to think of a poem,
That sounds really cool.

Looking round the classroom,
Thinking what to do,
Looking at the planets,
*I know what to do!*

Jupiter is orange,
Saturn a yellowy-brown,
Mars the colour of a red velvet cushion,
In the Queen's best crown.

Venus is a greeny-brown,
Mercury white, black and grey,
Earth from above is green and blue,
White and the colour of hay.

Uranus is turquoise,
Neptune a beautiful blue,
But what colour is Pluto? I don't know, do you?
I'm looking at the posters,
On the classroom wall,
On some it's blue, on some it's grey,
On some it's no colour at all.

What colour is Pluto? I really need to know,
Is it the colour of lush green grass
Or white like winter snow?

After a long conclusion, I think that you'll agree too,
Out of all the colours that I've seen,
I think that Pluto's *blue!*

**Halla Price  (10)**
**Tarland Primary School, Tarland**

# If I Were A Planet

If I were a planet I'd definitely be Pluto,
Bright, bouncy and blue.
Halla would be Neptune,
Beautiful, quiet and new.

Megan would be Jupiter,
King of all that rule,
Amanda would be Saturn,
Queen of the swimming pool.

Katie would be Venus,
Cool, casual but neat.
Selena would be Mars,
Sugary, shiny and sweet.

Stacey would be Earth,
Full of life and joy.
Abbie would be Uranus,
Playing with her toys.

Mrs Gibb would be the sun,
Fiery-tempered and all!
Claire would be Mercury,
In the dinner hall.

**Ellie Palmer (10)**
**Tarland Primary School, Tarland**


# Roses

Roses, roses oh how I do love roses,
In all colours and shapes that they come in,
But out of all the roses that I've seen
I think that I like red,
Pink is very pretty, so is white, but when
I get married I think I'll have red.

**Ishbel Rosie Price (8)**
**Tarland Primary School, Tarland**

# Colours

Colours, colours, colours,
I'm mad about colours.

Red is rusty or bright with glee,
Yellow is yellow like a bumblebee,
Green is a colour that's nice and plain,
Blue's gone completely insane.

Purple is the sunset,
Orange the velvet on the bedset,
Pink is a pinky pink,
The colour of the pink sink.

Brown the colour of our shaggy dog,
You'll see black even in fog,
But imagine if these colours were one,
But imagine if they were stuck on the sun.

**Emer Cunningham (8)**
**Tarland Primary School, Tarland**

# Snail

S lippery slimy snail
N oiseless as anything
A nnoying everyone's food
I nching across the path
L ying in the sand.

**Arlene Jenkins (8)**
**Tarland Primary School, Tarland**

# Slug

S limy small slug,
L ittle small silly slug,
U pon a small cloud in the sky,
G um stuck on a slug.

**Sarah Preston (8)**
**Tarland Primary School, Tarland**

# Sea Creatures

Dolphins rule,
Dolphins are cool,
Dolphins should not be kept in a swimming pool,
Because it is cruel.

Sharks are blue, grey or white,
They must stay out of sight,
To catch some fish
And put in a dish.

Whales are white, blue or grey,
They do not eat hay
But they like to play,
On a Tuesday.

They wag their tails,
Males or females,
All sizes and shapes,
But they are not apes.

**Jade Whitaker  (9)**
**Tarland Primary School, Tarland**

# My Friends

M  y friends are very kind,
Y  our friends keep you happy when you're down.

F  orever and ever you should be friends,
R  est and in peace,
I  love having friends,
E  ndless friendship,
N  ever ever, friendliness will never
D  ie away,
S  ince we are still friends.

**Megan Andrew  (10)**
**Victoria Primary School, Airdrie**

# Sean

S  is for Scotland, the country he lives in now,
E  is for England, the country he used to live in,
A  is for the second letter in happy which Sean is a lot,
N  is for nippy when Sean is cold.

T  is for temper which Sean has a lot of,
A  is for angry which Sean gets a lot,
R  is for red which is Sean's favourite colour,
P  is for Patrick, his middle name,
L  is for line monitor that he does after we play,
E  is for educated guy, he is very smart,
E  is for example which Sean gives to the younger pupils.

**George Gordon  (10)**
**Victoria Primary School, Airdrie**


# World War Two

Children were taken away,
Mothers and children kept together,
People were gassed and left to rot,
Families split up,
Destruction everywhere.

The war was horrible,
Adolph Hitler the leader of the Nazis,
Wanted to kill the Jewish race,
Together the Jews fought
And won.
Hopefully another won't occur,
Because it destroyed too many families.

**Chloe Robertson  (11)**
**Victoria Primary School, Airdrie**

## Drugs And Smoking

Don't take drugs because they are bad,
If you do you'll make your life real sad,
If you smoke a cigarette,
Don't because you will regret.

If you take coke or smack,
Don't because you won't get your life back,
If you take a syringe,
You just might do stupid things.

If the police catch you with it,
You'll get put in jail,
You'll be in for about four years,
So you'll not get a career.

Some people think drugs are cool,
At the end of it they're making their lives miserable,
So don't take drugs, get a wife
And live a happy life.

**Craig Lafferty  (11)**
**Victoria Primary School, Airdrie**


## Billy Bob

B illy Bob is so disgusting,
 I mitation is his thing. Messing about. Ah he's revolting.
L ooking at me with his spotty face,
L urking about with no grace
Y ou may think he looks nice but trust me he's *not!*

B oys, boys, oh goodness me!
O ut growing legs, oh find me a cup of tea!
B illy Bob, oh I hate him!

**Amy Priest  (11)**
**Victoria Primary School, Airdrie**

# Football

Football mad, football crazy,
Football all the way,
Football is the best,
We can never get away,
My friends and I play it every day.

I want to be a football player,
I want to be a star,
I want to play every day,
I want to play with my friends before I go too far.

**Gordon Allan  (10)**
**Victoria Primary School, Airdrie**


# My Family

F amily
A re always there for you,
M ake you do your chores
 I n your house and in your room.
L isten to your music while you are working,
Y esterday I forgot to do my chores and I got shouted at.

**Kerri Smith  (11)**
**Victoria Primary School, Airdrie**


# Friends And Family

F riends and family,
A re always there for you when you need them most,
M emories will always be treasured,
 I n family people will always be remembered,
L ove and care will be used with each other,
Y awning in the cold winter morning.

**Cherise Devlin  (11)**
**Victoria Primary School, Airdrie**

# Mum

M um is someone you love when you're little,
   You call her Mummy.
   She is always there for you and gives you lots of money.
U ps and downs we have but you always know how to
                            cheer me up.
M um, just one more thing to say, mums are the best but
   sometimes they really need time to rest.

**Robyn Longmuir  (11)**
**Victoria Primary School, Airdrie**


# Limos

L imos are long, limos are big,
I f you are ever in one you will think they are great,
M iraculous they are, as cool as a star,
O ut of your mind, there's lots of different kinds,
S hiny and bright, they're easy to sight.

**David Moylan  (11)**
**Victoria Primary School, Airdrie**


# Dancing

D ancing is my hobby
A nyone can do it
N ever knowing when you're going to stop
C heerleading and majorette
I mportant times to pay attention
N ever stop moving and …
G rooving to the music!

**Chelsea Marshall  (11)**
**Victoria Primary School, Airdrie**

## Thomas

T roublemaker number one
H appy as a bumblebee
O ver the hill laughing away because he is suspended
M ental as a monkey
A nnoying as a Dennis the Menace brother - *Help!*
S porty and loves playing and watching football.

**Ashley McNee  (11)**
**Victoria Primary School, Airdrie**

## Dancing

Dancing is so good,
The teachers are so cool,
They teach us new dances,
Every day and they are good.

Some teachers teach ballet,
Some teach tap
And you never ever dance to rap.

**Paula Reid  (11)**
**Victoria Primary School, Airdrie**

## George

G eorge is my friend no matter what,
E ven though he talks a lot,
O nly at school I see him be,
R ed is his favourite colour, the same as me,
G eorge is the best friend I've ever had,
E ven though he's sometimes sad.

**Sean Tarplee  (11)**
**Victoria Primary School, Airdrie**

# My Family

In my family there is my sister, Mum, Dad and pet,
Thankfully we have never taken her to the vet.

My sister is well … a bit dumb,
But if I said it out aloud, I would get a row from my mum.

My mum is kind and sweet,
She is a real treat.

My dad is dead funny,
He is very happy and sunny.

And my pet hamster, Pickles, is the best pet ever,
She is very, very clever.

**Lauren McLeod  (11)**
**Victoria Primary School, Airdrie**